Traditional
Indian
Textiles

JOHN GILLOW AND NICHOLAS BARNARD
Traditional Indian Textiles

With 195 illustrations, 169 in colour, and 4 maps

THAMES AND HUDSON

To the memory of my late father, J.G. Gillow

Our thanks to: Peter Ackroyd, Janet Anderson, Elizabeth
Andrews, Tim Ashfield, Karen and Alan Beagle, Ishwar
Singh Bhatti, Kay Brooks, Peter Collingwood, Ilay Cooper,
Dennis Cope, Rosemary Crill, S.N. Das, Rosie Ford,
Gilubhai, Janet Harvey, Celia Herrick, Jennie Parry, the late
Manubhai, Radakishan Maheshweri and family, Abdul
Sattar Meghani and family, James Merrell, Anne Morell,
M-L. Nabholtz-Kartaschoff, Aithur Muni Krishnan, Julia
Nicholson, Sheila Paine, D. Paparao, Khodidas Parmar,
Rose and Nelson Rands, Khatri S. Salehmohmad Parvani,
Bharat Patadia, Karen Scadeng, Khatri Mohammed Siddiq,
John Smith, Rabu and Munji Sharma, Meira Stockl,
Marianne Straub, Judy Turner, Badal Uttam, Motabhai
Vadya, Piers Vitebski, and Goodie and Amrit Vohra.

Frontispiece: Child's cap piece, Kutch

Printed and bound in Singapore
by Singapore National Printers Ltd

Contents

Introduction

Fifteen years ago, after one of those long, dusty, apparently endless train journeys so typical of India, I alighted at last at Bhuj railway station in the far north-west of the country.

There I looked on to a walled, gated town, whose incongruous centrepiece is a Victorian Gothic tower – part of the Maharao's palace, but better fitted to a public school in the English countryside. I walked through the main bazaar of Bhuj, past silver merchants and shops full to bursting with fine mashru satins and shawls. Jostling past me came Sidis of African descent, as well as Ahir and Rabari, Hindu herders in their mirrorwork costumes and ivory bangles, and Kanbi farming women with chain-stitch blouses and skirts. Stalking through them all came tall and lean Jat Muslim herders, henna-bearded men in ajarakh block-printed turbans and lungis, and women wearing profusely embroidered tunics, heavy gold nose-rings and madder-dyed bandhani shawls and skirts. Here were communities and castes living side by side, at peace – and expressing their differences through colour and textiles.

In the workshops, I saw block printers and bandhani workers, weavers at pitlooms producing mashru satins and dablo blankets for the herders and farmers. Later, in the villages, I saw interiors decorated with bead-work panels and hung with embroidered, pennanted bunting setting off highly polished brass pots and silverware, with furniture carved with the recurring patterns of flowers, birds and animals, all against walls decorated with a relief of mud sculpture, whitewashed and inset with mirrors.

No other land enjoys such a profusion of creative energies for the production of textiles as the subcontinent of India. The interaction of peoples – invaders, indigenous tribes, traders and explorers – has built a complex culture legendary for its vitality and colour; today, over ten million weavers, dyers, embroiderers and spinners contribute their handmade textiles to this melting pot.

From earliest trading records, it is clear that European, Asian and Levantine civilizations looked to India for her textiles. Greeks, Romans, Arabs, Persians and Chinese traded precious metals and silks for the fine and colourful cottons of the Subcontinent. The special quality of the light cotton cloth, the embroidery techniques, the ability to respond with alacrity and sensitivity to the demands for new designs and patterns, as well as the fast nature of the colourful dyes, ensured that, until the European Industrial Revolution, India was the world's foremost centre of textile production.

Today, India has more than recovered from the disasters wrought by the flood of foreign powerloom imports. From the Rann of Kutch to the Coromandel Coast and from city to village the handloom weavers, block printers, textile painters, dyers and embroiderers work to continue the developing traditions of Indian textiles crafts. *Traditional Indian Textiles* focuses on the twentieth-century development of this home and small workshop industry. The histories of textile traditions are examined, the techniques of dyeing, weaving and embroidering are analysed and the country is traversed from region to region to explore and highlight the centres of traditional textile production. For the designer, traveller, student and collector, *Traditional Indian Textiles* is the essential guide to the most famous of all crafts of the Subcontinent.

John Gillow

1 The History of Textile Production

The production of sophisticated textiles within the Indian subcontinent has prehistoric origins. Yet though we are spoilt with riches from other cultures with a less fecund weaving history – from the ancient Central Asian and pre-Columbian weavers and embroiderers, for instance, whose work has been stored in the cryogenically sealed tombs of the Siberian Altai, or the desiccated burial troves of the Peruvian coastal desert, tragically none of the wealth of ancient Indian textile manufacture has survived. In fact, the unpredictable patterns of the extremes of the alternately wet and dry climate have ensured that only a few fragments of bio-degradable woven plant and animal fibre remain to help us chart with any degree of accuracy the history of Indian textiles. This lack of tangible evidence is counterbalanced in part by an abundance of archaeological finds and literary references that have, at times, transported the quest for analytical and accurate data into a world of delightful myths and legends that are very much more in keeping with the mystical and religious qualities still associated with traditional Indian textiles.

The earliest textile finds were made at Mohenjo-daro, an archaeological site of the third millennium BC on the Indus River. There, woven and madder-dyed cotton fragments wrapped round a silver pot had been preserved by the metallic salts that impregnated the cloth. The use of madder dye made fast with a mordant and the presence of dye vats at the site testify to an advanced understanding of the processes of colour fixing on cloth, and a relief-carved stone sculpture from the dig clearly depicts figures draped with patterned cloth. Spindles were found at Mohenjo-daro and used, most probably, to wind weft threads when working at a wooden loom; the presence of bronze needles at the site suggests that this Bronze-Age civilization embellished its woven cloth with embroidery or supplementary threadwork on the loom. From this evidence we may surmise that some peoples of the Subcontinent were at least two, perhaps

three, millennia in advance of the European world in the preparation and use of cotton and mordanted dyestuffs.

Aside from the tapestry-cloth discoveries in Central Asia at the tombs in the Altai mountains (6th–4th centuries BC) and in Turkestan (2nd century BC–10th century AD), some of which may be of Indian origin, no examples of cloth from the Subcontinent were known until the copious nineteenth-century finds of trade cloth unearthed at Fostat, near Cairo in Egypt, some of which date back to the fifteenth century. We have both Asian and European literary references to cloth production to shed light on the many centuries bridging these archaeological finds. Assyrian and Babylonian tablets from the seventh century BC allude to the cotton cloth trade between Mesopotamia and the Subcontinent. From within India itself the Hindu epics such as the *Ramayana* and the *Mahabharata*, as well as Buddhist sources, chart in detail the processes and uses of textiles made of cotton, linen and silk between the fifteenth and the second centuries BC. The silk yarn is thought to be Chinese, suggesting the existence of a long-established overland trading route with the lands north of the Himalayas. By the sixth century BC the expansion of the Persian Empire linked the Indus basin with the Mediterranean by overland and coastal trade routes. Indian cloth became much coveted by both the Persians and the Greeks because of its brilliant colours.

The empire of Alexander the Great and his colonizing Greek successors extended to the foothills of the Hindu Kush. Alexander's invasion of India in 327 BC and his two years of campaigning encouraged cultural and trading links that reached from Asia Minor and the Mediterranean sea ports to India by way of land routes through Persia and Afghanistan. Such links were strengthened by a regular exchange of envoys continuing through three generations of Seleucid and Mauryan kings. Such was the consistency and continuity of commerce through this early period that textile and other trading networks soon radiated from the ports of western and eastern India. Goods flowed to and from the peninsula of India both overland and by coastal sea routes, and from India to Ceylon and Burma by way of the ports of Orissa and Bengal. Trade with China was established through the eastern route traversing Assam and Burma. To the west, the lands of Arabia, Persia, Mesopotamia, Asia Minor and the Mediterranean were linked by coastal trading stations on the Arabian and Red Seas to the Gulf of Cambay. The Arabian Sea was crossed by pioneering Arab sailors, who used accurate stellar navigation throughout the monsoon-blown summer voyage from west to east. They would then remain in India until the opposite winter winds allowed them to return to the ports of Aden and Socotra. These sea routes carried the main bulk of trade between the Mediterranean world and the Subcontinent.

By 250 BC, the marauding activities of the nomadic tribes north of the Himalayas set the scene for the establishment of a trade route that was to assume a title more of romantic than economic importance – the Silk Route. Thwarted to the east by the Great Wall, pasture-seeking tribes ventured west and south, displacing the

'Moti' (beadwork) 'chakla' (square hanging)

Scythians from the Aral Sea hinterland. The Scythians, in turn, moved into Bactria and Parthia, bringing Central Asia into the Indian trading world and laying the foundations for the Silk Route. Indian traders carried commerce to the remote

towns of Kashgar, Khotan, Turfan and Yarkand, establishing merchant colonies and a new era of communication with China. In the West, the wealthy Roman Empire sought out the luxury goods of the East, and Indian merchants became both middlemen and suppliers to this trade. The Roman demand for spice encouraged Indians to travel and trade further afield in South-East Asia, to Java and Sumatra, which eventually led to the establishment of sea-trading routes with China. By way of Indian traders spices, jewels, exotic animals, cotton and silk goods and silk yarn from China found an eager and rich Mediterranean consumer. Consequently, Rome developed a trade deficit with the East which, Pliny complained, caused a drain of over 550 million sesterces of gold bullion each year. By the first century AD, Gangetic Indian muslins were well known in Europe, lyrically described as 'venti' (fine as the wind) and 'nebula' (misty in nature).

Roman traders were to be found in south and west India and at one settlement, Arikamedu, on the south-east coast, it is known that muslins were woven to the requirements of the consumer some three thousand miles to the west. The *Periplus Maris Erythreae* of the first century AD, a maritime analysis of the regional trade, describes in detail the weaving centres of the Subcontinent, revealing the existence of a network of specialized trades little changed some two thousand years later. From the east coast came cotton, silk and indigo, with the finest muslins from the Gangetic delta; from the west coast, cotton, silk textiles and yarn.

This direct trade with a Mediterranean empire was to be halted by the notorious Huns of Central Asia. Thwarted in their advances to the east and south by the empires of China and India, the Huns turned westwards to destroy the Roman Empire. By the end of the fifth century they had penetrated north-central India and in their wake arrived other Central Asian tribes who were to assume cultural and military significance in the centuries to follow. By the end of the sixth century the Hunnish attacks ceased and the Persians and Turks took Bactria; Indian trade was now directed towards South-East Asia and amongst the large regional markets of India itself. Silk was imported from China in quantity, and Indian traders settled in Canton and throughout Thailand, Cambodia and the Indonesian archipelago, irrevocably influencing the religious and cultural development of each land.

Sinarth Brahmins wearing 'dhotis' (loin cloths). One holds a 'gaumukhi' – an embroidered glove, which contains the sacred prayer beads.

The famous Ajanta wall paintings of the fifth to the eighth centuries AD provide an invaluable record of the refined nature of the Indian textile industries of the time. The cave frescoes clearly depict dancers, nobles, servants and musicians clothed in loin cloths and blouses, most probably patterned by the resist techniques of printing, tie and dye and ikat as well as brocade weaving. By contrast to this picture of a world of the courtly rich in ceremonial attire, the two seventh-century Chinese pilgrims Yuang Chwang and I Tsing noted on their travels through India that the everyday costume of the people was not tailored and was mostly white. Reference is also made to the variation in garb between the wealthy and the poor, and to the clothing of the priestly classes.

Known for their adventurous seafaring spirit, the Arabs who came to western India at the beginning of the eighth century were fired by religious and territorial ambitions, and by a desire to control the lucrative spice trade with South-East Asia, until now in the hands of Indian middlemen. For more than two centuries, after the forcible conversion of the Zoroastrian Persians, the extension of the Muslim Empire into India was restricted to the occupation of Sind; however, the Arab traders succeeded, by settling permanently on the Malabar coast, in gaining control of the flow of sea trade between South-East Asia, India, the Mediterranean and beyond, which they then maintained for over seven hundred years.

The peace of this inward-looking interlude was irrevocably shattered from AD 998 onwards, when Mahmud of Ghanzi and his Afghan army conducted near-annual incursions into northern and central India to loot and break up the idols of the Hindu temples, returning laden with bullion, jewels and statues of precious metals. The eventual settling of north and central India by Turkish and Afghan sultans by the late twelfth century created the Delhi Sultanate, a regime that sponsored the arts with lavish displays of court patronage. The skills of weaving, textile production and decoration must by this time have reached a certain zenith, for a sultan would bestow robes of honour, numbering some hundreds of thousands of garments each year, upon his acolytes. A Delhi royal silk 'karkhanah' (workshop) is recorded as having employed over four thousand weavers to supply part of this ostentatious display of wealth, and the silk trade with Central Asia and China certainly flourished during this time, both overland and by Arab-

North Indian portrait of a man and boy proudly wearing Kashmir shawls with resist-dyed turbans

The dying years of the fifteenth century and the early decades of the sixteenth were to be most significant for the Subcontinent. Culturally and commercially, the peoples of India were to be influenced by two totally different expansionist empires. After Vasco da Gama's discovery of the Cape of Good Hope route in 1498, the Portuguese were to found the first European coastal colonies in India at about the time the Mughals were establishing their northern kingdom. Whereas the Mughals confined their activities to mainland India, however, the Portuguese and other European nations not only formed new local powers within the region, but also set out to take over the lucrative Arab-controlled sea trade routes.

The primary driving force for European expansionism was the value of spice, an essential flavouring and preservative for meat. High profits could be made from this commodity, and other factors, such as a popular anti-Muslim sentiment, the disruption of overland trade links by the marauding Central Asian tribes and the desire to overturn the Venetian and Egyptian trade stranglehold, sent Columbus in one direction in 1492 and Vasco da Gama in the other, both seeking 'Christians and spices'. For a century, Portugal reaped the rewards of its commercial acumen; under Portuguese control, Malabar became the re-export centre for spices from the East Indies, and the maritime routes from the Arabian Sea to the Malaccan straits became a Portuguese domain. Toll was exacted from other sea trade by a system of licences.

Babur, the first leader of the Mughals, established a legendary empire, an interlude of independence between the foreign rule of the Central Asian Turks and the British. There have been few more opulent consumers of exotic weavings and embroideries than the Mughal nobility and their acolytes. Their copious patronage of the arts was in part a result of laws of inheritance, for assignments of land to the nobility lasted for life only and the next generation would have to scrabble upwards from the bottom once more; taxes remained in arrears until death, when a great man's property would be sealed and the remainder released after the deduction of exacting dues. It is no surprise, therefore, that the Mughal lords were profligate.

The glory and ostentation of this time are still evident throughout northern India. Public works projects were popular, mosques were built, wells excavated, retainers clothed, rest houses

controlled sea routes that linked the prosperous Indian and South-East Asian ports. Influences from western Asia and further afield are evident in the architecture of this period, when Afghans, Mongols, Turks, Persians, Arabs and Abyssinians were all drawn to the magnificent city and court of Delhi as craftsmen, soldiers and adventurers.

The two-hundred-year reign of the sultans ended in 1398 when Tamerlane sacked Delhi, and after a fifty-year period of recovery under the Sayyids the north of India returned to Afghan rule under the Lodis. The weakening of this regime by inter-tribal jealousies prompted the governors of the Punjab and Sind, in the second decade of the fifteenth century, to invite an adventurer from Central Asia to help assert their independence and re-establish their status within the Sultanate. An appeal for assistance to Babur, a direct descendant of Tamerlane and Genghis Khan, proved to be an unwise move, for at the battle of Panipat in 1526 the Afghans were defeated and Babur then founded a dynasty that was to rule India as the magnificent Mughal Empire.

established and summer palaces and gardens lovingly created. Textiles of woven and brocaded precious metal threads were fastidiously worked in the royal workshops, palaces were caparisoned with colourful hangings and whole tented cities travelled with the royal court when the emperor was campaigning, hunting or surveying his dominion. Royal workshops and local village outworkers satisfied the needs of the nobility — François Tavernier, a traveller who in 1665 visited the karkhanahs of the court, noted that artisans such as weavers, embroiderers and wood turners, as well as painters and lacquering specialists, were each given the use of a large hall, within which they practised their craft.

External trade flourished during the seventeenth century — the golden years of the Mughal Empire — and, as the Romans had previously discovered, the drain of bullion to the Subcontinent from Europe was a cause for serious Western concern. Textiles, indigo, saltpetre and spices were sent westwards, and exchanged for wine, novelties, horses and precious metals. The fine colouring, patterning, weaving and dye-fast properties of Indian cloth delighted the Western consumer and from the early days of the Portuguese incursions the printed, painted and embroidered cloths were in great demand. The textile production was further stimulated by the almost simultaneous arrival of the Dutch and the English in Southern Asia, their goal being to break the Portuguese stranglehold on the spice trade. The first Dutch fleet of 1595 sailed directly to the source of the precious commodity, establishing a new colony in Batavia (now Jakarta), in Java. The Dutch established a cunning network of trade in which India became a key link as a source of inexpensive fine textiles. With cheap cloth bought in India, the Dutch were able to barter for valuable spices in the East Indies without having to draw on their scarce reserves of silver. Their merchants prospered greatly by this triangular trade and found south India valuable not only for textiles but for its own supply of pepper, cardamom and cinnamon.

The English were too late to grasp direct control of the East Indies, and so they looked to India as a possible alternative. Established on 31 December 1600, the East India Company initiated a steady rather than heady pattern of trade between the East and Europe. From west India, and particularly from Gujarat, came embroideries, printed cloth and indigo, and from the Malabar

Rajasthani women, dressed in richly decorated traditional garb: a brocade 'odhni' (shawl) with 'mashru' border; and (right) a 'bandhani' (tie-and-dye) odhni.

coast, the spices of the East Indies and Ceylon; Madras and the south-east was a source of cottons, Kashmir produced a now legendary supply of shawls, and Bengal sugar, silks, embroideries and fine muslins. In return India purchased metals, novelties and ivory. The broadcloth of the English was of no interest to the Indians, and so the imbalance of trade had again to be redressed with silver bullion.

Some idea of the scale, range and wealth of Indian textile exports from the fifteenth century onwards has been confirmed by the Fostat finds in Egypt and from well-preserved collections of furnishing cloth within the stately homes of Europe. In Egypt, the Arab city of Fostat was built near Cairo after the defeat of the Byzantines in AD 641, and was to become one of the great entrepôts of the Arab world. The remnants of the throughflow of trade textiles were discovered first of all in the nineteenth century, and great quantities of Coptic tapestry weavings as well as printed cloth from Gujarat have since been unearthed by archaeological excavations. The oldest of these fragments have been dated as fifteenth century or earlier and, although none may be classed as luxury cloth, the sophistication of the resist printing and dyeing techniques is still evident despite the ravages of time. Influences in design range from Muslim and Hindu to styles drawn from the European tradition. The cloth was probably destined for use as garment material, household furnishings and religious covers or hangings.

The flexibility and creativity of the Indian weavers and embroiderers in their commercial response to both export and domestic trends is well documented, therefore, from ancient times. And from the seventeenth century to the present day there are many surviving examples of cloth that clearly emphasize the tremendous range of Indian cloth production and the Subcontinent's ability to cater for the export market: for the Europeans were produced prints, embroideries and quilts decorated with flower and animal designs; for the Muslims of East Africa and the Arabian peninsula more simple printed cloth as well as striped cotton and silk textiles; and for the Indonesian archipelago the extraordinary double-ikat cloth so cherished by the nobility. Certainly for many centuries India had been trading via the Levant to the Mediterranean, to supply the demands for fine furnishing cloth, and to the East by sea, for the Indonesian market; but it was the trading companies of the French, Dutch, Portuguese and English who kindled the fires of greater export production. At first the printed calicoes were treated as bartering cloth for spice, but by the seventeenth century their value in the European market was realized, and by the early 1700s, surveys were commissioned to determine the types, designs, colours and quantity of cloth suitable for the consumer. Chinese and South-East Asian designs were introduced, mingling with Mughal, Persian and Hindu traditions. Embroideries from Gujarat and Bengal and painted cloths from the east coast depicted idyllic scenes of arboreal, floral and bird life, intertwined to charming effect. 'Pintathoe', from the Portuguese 'pintado' meaning 'painted', was the descriptive term for much of east Indian decorated calico. Later the painted cloths were known as 'chintes', from the Hindi 'chint' meaning 'variegated'. By the late seventeenth century, this term was applied to both painted and printed cloth, eventually spawning the English word 'chintz'.

To the east, the trade production included the Bengali embroideries and quilts, which were produced with a dramatic visual intermingling of cultures, featuring European heraldry and direct pictorial representation of local and foreign peoples and wildlife, as well as a mêlée of Hindu and Christian religious themes. By the early years of the nineteenth century the great demand for clothing and furnishing fabrics favoured the block-printing production methods, at the expense of the embroiderers and painters of textiles. The weaving communities that had, by the end of the nineteenth century, entered a longterm and irreversible decline include the producers of specialist textile trading commodities such as the intricately dyed and finely woven patola and mashru cloths of Gujarat. Each was destined for a particular market, the patola to Indonesia for court attire and the mashru to the Muslim communities of East and West Africa, as well as of the Arabian peninsula and the Levant.

Of greater fame than the printed, painted and embroidered cloth, and especially in more recent decades, is the Kashmir shawl. Always a luxury commodity, the tapestry-woven fine wool shawl had become a fashion wrap for the ladies of the English and French élite by the late eighteenth century. As early as 1803 Kashmiri needlework production was established to hasten output, and even earlier, in 1784, the English had begun to weave imitation Kashmir shawls. Other Europeans, notably the French, soon followed the English example. But by 1870, the widespread use of the semi-mechanized Jacquard loom in Europe destroyed the exclusivity of the Kashmir shawl, causing a catastrophic collapse of indigenous manufacture.

Having arrived to trade, the English increasingly took a hold on the reins of government, a process that was set in motion by Robert Clive's conquest of Bengal in 1757. This was consolidated in the next hundred years with the spread of British rule over most of the Subcontinent, and then brought to fruition as the all-powerful British Raj of the late nineteenth century. Certainly the policy towards trade remained constant, with the Subcontinent seen as a developing market for the goods run off from the newly mechanized workshops of industrialized Britain. The English continued to import specialist embroideries and painted and printed cloth for an ever-changing and prospering society, and had taken up their new scientific tools to perfect the techniques of

Contemporary 'kantha' (quilted and embroidered) panel

spinning cotton as well as those of dyeing and printing, later to apply such ideas to the development of the cloth-printing machine. By the early nineteenth century the sheds of Lancashire, resounding with the din of textile mass production, had machines reeling off finely printed and fast-coloured cotton yardage with designs specifically created for the Indian market.

For the Indian textile handicrafts industry, the first seventy years of the nineteenth century were dismal, as it suffered from the influx of cheap English cloth. In response to this trend, and against a powerful English protectionist lobby, the first mechanized cotton mill was established in India in 1854. By the turn of the century, having capitalized on the disruption of North American cotton supplies during their Civil War, the Indian cotton mills flourished, dominating the economies of the cities of Bombay and Ahmedabad. The crippling protectionist legislation in favour of the English mills was abandoned in 1925 and the development of the industry since Independence has confirmed India's position as a major exporter of machine-loomed cloth.

In the struggle to achieve independence from the British, Mahatma Gandhi seized upon the idea of using the domestic weaving industry as a symbol to bring home to the people the reality and implications of commercial domination by foreign rulers. 'Khadi' (cloth handwoven from indigenous handspun cotton) was the symbol of a homespun independence and self-sufficiency within the village unit. This khadi program has reinvigorated the handloom industry of India, directly inspiring highly successful commercial developments such as co-operatives of production and marketing throughout the traditional weaving, printing and painted textile centres and states of India.

In addition to this village, town and city power- and hand-produced textile manufacture, there is the domestic decoration of cloth by women of such groups as the shepherds, gypsies and farmers of the more remote regions of the Subcontinent. Amongst these peoples, the embellishment of traditional fabrics by fine embroidery and the imaginative use of appliqué techniques is a part of everyday life. The richest source for this type of production is undoubtedly the north-west of India.

The traditions of cloth manufacture within India continue to develop, and the production of handmade textiles is flourishing, perhaps as never before. Very little has changed over the centuries of international trade. As ever, there are so many levels and types of production, some on the one hand developing and copying from all sources to match the vagaries of taste of the domestic and export market, while yet others continue to produce textiles for traditional family purposes. Truly, India remains the most original, creative and prolific source of textile production in the world.

2 The Materials

As we have seen, one of the fundamental reasons for the continuing success of Indian textile manufacture over the centuries has been its ability to cope with a broad range of market demands. Indian weavers, dyers and embroiderers have been guided by merchants, other middlemen and more recently by government craft societies to produce textiles that might be best described as 'tailored for market preference'. This flexibility of production, combined with the energy of a largely traditional Indian craft society, has resulted in the outpouring of textiles with an enormous variety of colours, patterns and textures.

Of all the textile crafts, it is for the art of dyeing that the Indian peoples have been world-famous for many centuries, and especially for their processing of natural dyestuffs and application of fast dyes with which to decorate cloth.

Dyes

The dyers of the Subcontinent have been creating fast colours for textile decoration for a very long time, at least since the second millennium BC. The secrets of the technical skills that form the core of the dyers' art were not discovered by the West until the seventeenth century; and thus it was that for over three thousand years, the natives of Europe had to be content for the most part with dun-coloured woollen cloth, textiles of animal hair, furs and flax which, when decorated, would be no more than painted or daubed with fugitive colours of vegetable, animal and mineral origin. The fast dyeing or bright colour dyeing that did occur in the West was in the preparation of cloth for the aristocracy and the very wealthy; indeed, certain brilliant and rare colours were restricted to that use only. No wonder the ancient Greeks, their fellow Mediterraneans and the later European visitors to the Subcontinent were enraptured by the colourful cloth they found in common use: washable as well as colourful and colourfully patterned, it certainly seemed to display miraculous qualities for garment and furnishing cloth.

Primary evidence for the very early mordanting of cotton cloth for decoration is provided by the printed textile fragments found at the Mohenjo-daro excavations. The cotton plant is endemic to this area of the Indus Valley, which is thought to be one of the first regions to develop techniques for processing the fruit of the perennial wild cotton plant, *Gossypium arboreum*, from a boll of vegetable fibres to yarn ready to weave. Although such useful fibrous material was available in abundance, it was less adaptable than animal fibres such as sheep's wool, silk, horse, goat and camel hair, for it will not accept natural dyes for permanent colouring. From early on, therefore, it was necessary to find ways to develop and improve on dyestuffs which could be made to coat insolubly, or 'bind' on to, the surface of the cotton fibres.

The secret of this fast colouring of vegetable fibres lay in sensitive and intelligent use of metal oxides as an intermediary substance. Such a substance is known as 'mordant', a word derived from the Latin 'mordere', meaning 'to bite'. The mordant 'bites' the fibre in combination with the dyestuff to fix the colour. There are over three hundred dye-yielding plants endemic to the Indian subcontinent which, after careful preparation, can be used with the various types, densities and qualities of mordants.

The application and significance of colour is central to the Hindu culture, as the textile scholar Pupul Jayakar made clear in an article published in the magazine *Marg* (XV,4,1962): 'In India the sensitivity to colour has expressed itself in painting, poetry, music, and in the costumes worn both by peasant and emperor. Raga was the word used both for mood and dye. Colours were surcharged with nuances of mood and poetic

Bengali women arrayed in jamdani and brocade saris

association. Red was the colour evoked between lovers: a local Hindi couplet enumerates three tones of red, to evoke the three states of love; of these, manjitha, madder, was the fastest, for like the dye, it could never be washed away. Yellow was the colour of Vasant, of spring, of young mango blossoms, of swarms of bees, of southern winds and the passionate cry of mating birds. Nila, indigo, was the colour of Krishna, who is likened to a rain-filled cloud. But there is another blue, Hari nila, the colour of water in which the sky is reflected. Gerua, saffron, was the colour of the earth and of the yogi, the wandering minstrel, the seer and the poet who renounces the earth. These colours when worn by peasant or emperor were but a projection of the moods evoked by the changing seasons. The expression of mood through colour and dress was considered of such consequence that special colours were prescribed to be worn by a love-sick person and a person observing a vow.'

The craftworkers who have been responsible for creating and reproducing this panoply of dye colours have never enjoyed the lofty status of their patrons. Despite their specialist and often highly prized skills, remuneration has ever been modest. Working as extended family groups, dyers remain locked within the caste system at the lower levels of the social and economic scale. National and local government bodies have in recent years, however, endeavoured with some success to give greater appreciation, respect and financial rewards to select members of so venerable a craft industry by instituting awards and titles of rank for the dyers. For the most part, however, their lot is to remain in as limited a sphere of social opportunity as their predecessors. Seventeenth-century descriptions of the activities

'Chakla' (square hanging)

of dyeing communities tally with the practices of today, whereby specific trade cloth and dyestuffs are allocated to families with an order, on a piecework or outworker basis. Communities of the same caste within a village or town will practise similar tasks or contribute various elements of production, eventually creating the type of textile for which that area is famous. Other castes may well practise yet more specialized or different traditional dyeing and textile-decorating work within the same district. In every instance, however, both young and old participate in the textile dyeing as a matter of course, allocated specific tasks according to status or experience.

Whatever their standards of living, the dyers of India are ensured pride of place in the world history of the textile arts. Until the late nineteenth century, they worked exclusively with natural dyes. An aura of reverence and respect for the properties of these dyes permeated their lives and, even after the discovery of the chief chemical dyes by the Western producers, the Indian dyers claimed that their indigenous and naturally occurring dye substances not only lasted longer but strengthened, rather than harmed or weakened, the cloth. Yet, the introduction of these new chemical dyes in the 1890s dealt a body-blow to the traditional practices of the dyers and the final death knell to much of the farming of dye crops; it was said that it also 'injured the artistic feelings of the people and demoralized the indigenous crafts'.

Chemical dyes are a marketing dream: they can be used on all types of yarn, are relatively easy to handle and transport and above all, are cheap. Colour ranges may be selected from a chart and mixed, if desired; and neither supply nor price is subject to the vagaries of the monsoon climate which so bedevils the lives of the Indian farmers. Chemical dyes, therefore, are the primary source of colour for the textile industry of India in the twentieth century. Hampered at first by an inadequate understanding of the early aniline chemical dyes and their uses, bewildered by the range of bitingly bright colours available, the dyers of India laid themselves open to charges of declining aesthetic standards. Certainly the families and corporations involved in semi-mechanized and the more recent automated mass production of cloth have adopted chemical dyes to achieve an efficient and profitable output at the expense of the traditional aesthetic qualities of natural colours. In recent times the development and expert use of high quality and fine colour chrome dyes has contributed in part to the renaissance of interest in the textiles of India for the fashion and furnishing market of the West.

In another area of textile production, this century has seen a re-invigoration of India's handloom textile industry. Government organizations have been formed to spread an awareness of new raw materials, production skills and marketing possibilities. The All India Handlooms Board was established in 1952, the Institutes of Handloom Technology and the Weavers Service Centres in 1955. These organizations, in league with National Marketing Societies and their associated state co-operatives, have championed the cause of the weavers in both the home and the export market, awarding medals each year for excellence of production. By supporting the senior craftworkers in this way, a respect for the traditions of the past can be engendered within the young apprentices.

There still exist pockets of production that have always retained traditional methods, through specific local demand, a lack of choice, an abundance of dyestuffs or a dearth of finance. Communities of dyers and printers in Gujarat and Rajasthan produce distinctive printed 'ajarakh' cloth using both natural and chemical dyes. On the east coast the 'kalamkari' (pen-work) cloth printers and painters use both types of dyestuff sources: indigo is in prolific supply in the area, but their red shades come from chemical alizarin.

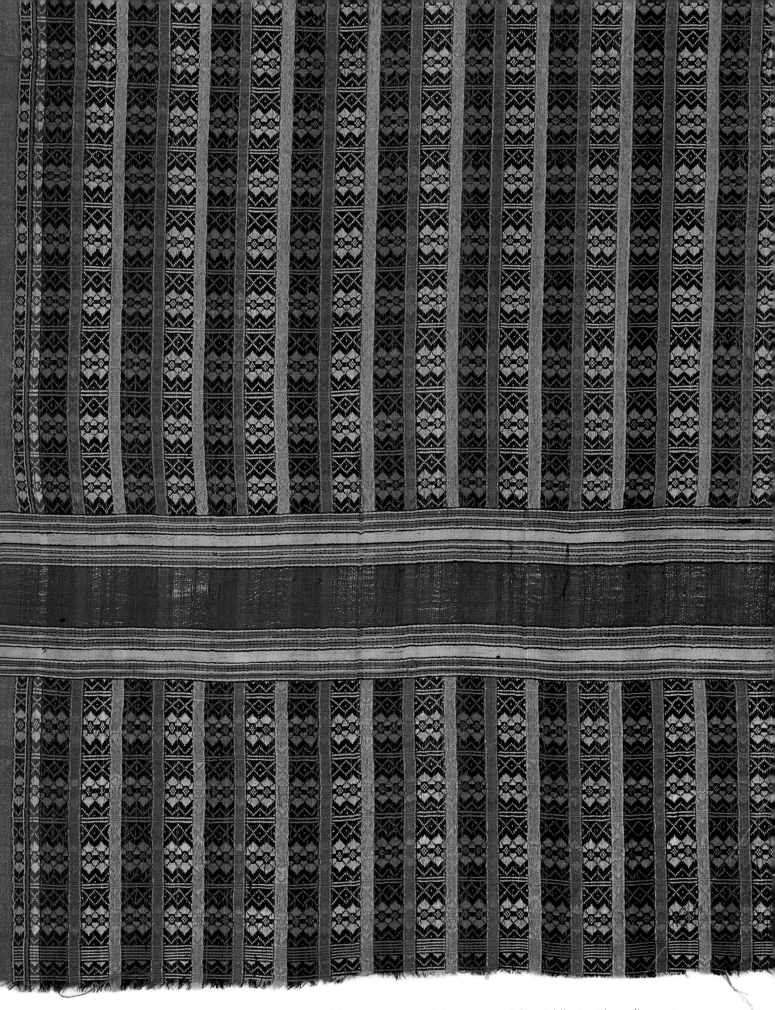

'Gulbadan' (a silk turban length) made of warp-faced brocade, worn by bridegrooms of the Maldhari cattle-trading castes in Sind, Banni Kutch and western Rajasthan. Multan, west Punjab, is the only surviving production centre. They were formerly woven in Sind.

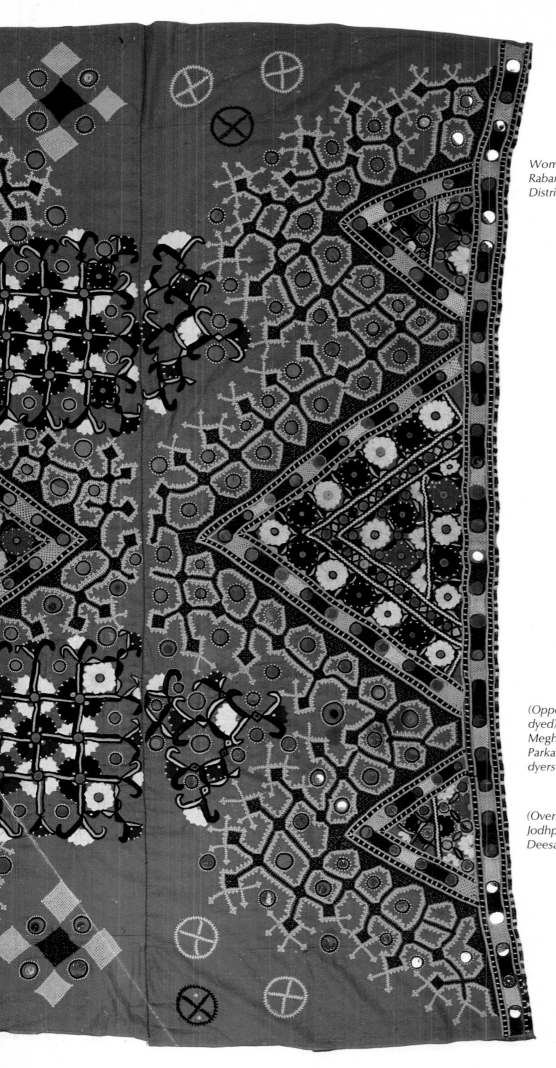

Woman's wedding 'odhni' (shawl) of the Rabari shepherd caste, from the Badin District of Sind

(Opposite) Sindhi 'bandhani' (tie-and-dyed) odhni, worn by the women of the Meghwal leather-workers caste of Thar Parkar, and made by the Hindu Khatri dyers of Khipro Sanghar, Sind

(Overleaf) Block-printed cloth lengths from Jodhpur or Jaisalmer, Rajasthan, and Deesa, Gujarat

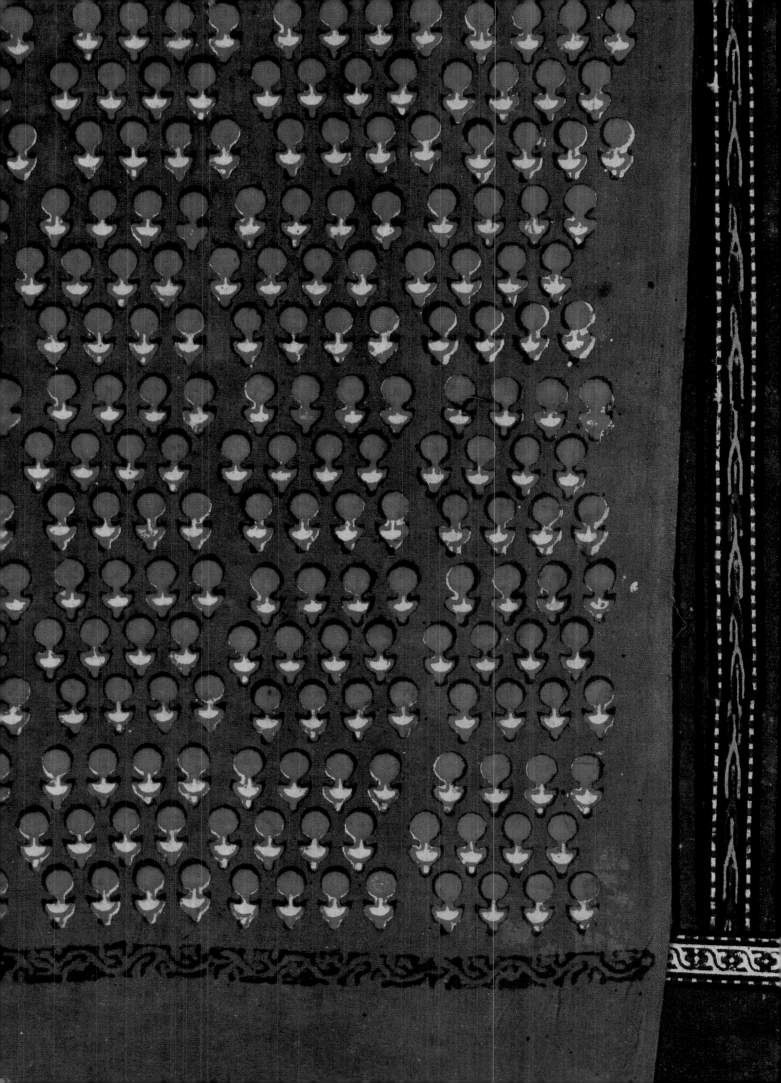

Single- and double-ikat sari in the Orissan style, but woven at Masulipatnam, Andhra Pradesh

Single-ikat bedsheet of cotton, from Nuapatna, Orissa

'Tangalia' (woollen loin cloth), worn by the women of the Bharwad herders of Saurashtra

(Opposite) Block-printed yardage from Bhairongarh, Madhya Pradesh

Nineteenth-century block-printed patterned sample cloth, intended for the Siamese market. From Gujarat.

(Overleaf) Ikat cotton lengths from Pochampalli, near Hyderabad, Andhra Pradesh. The cloths at the centre and to the right are of Japanese inspiration.

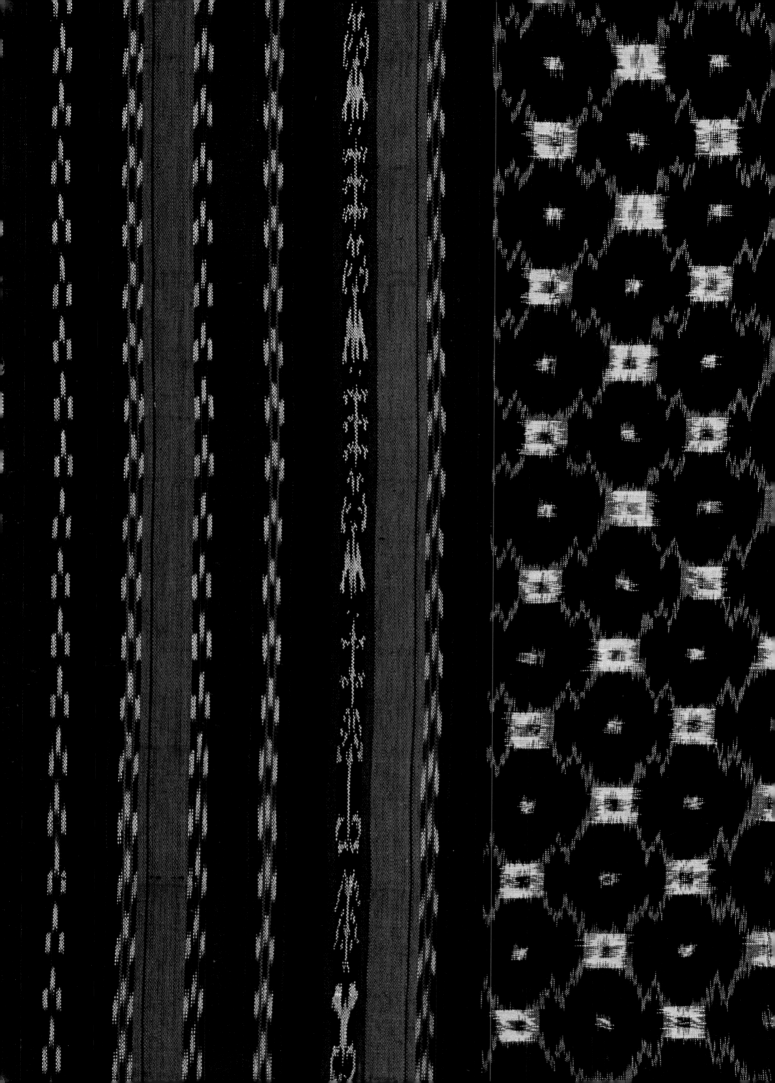

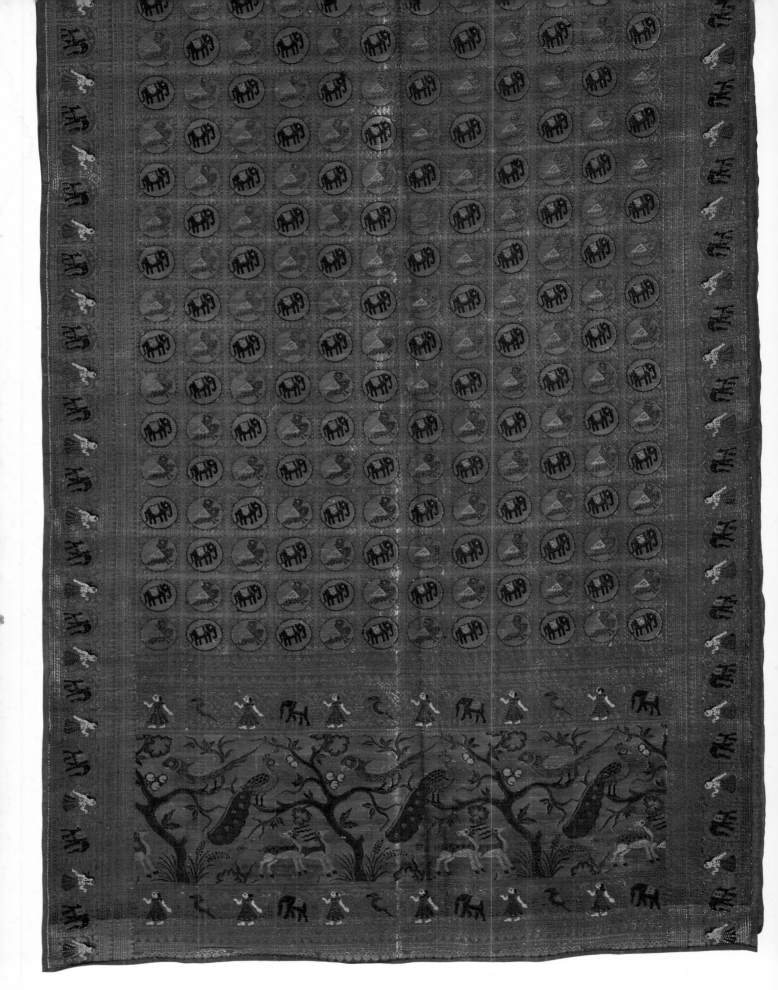

Brocade silk and metal threaded stole from Varanasi

Turban lengths from Jodhpur, Rajasthan, tie-and-dyed using the 'leheria' method

(Overleaf) Detail of single-ikat yardage made of wild silk yarn, from Nuapatna, Orissa

Natural Dyes

Natural dyes are either substantive or adjective. Substantive dyes need no mordant to fix the colour to the cloth fibre and sources include certain lichens, the bark and heartwood of trees and, most importantly, the indigo shrub, *Indigofera tinctoria*. Historically of great commercial value, this indigo species yields more than thirty times the quantity of the blue dye agent indican than the plants endemic to the West and further to the east. The indigo bush is found throughout India. At its peak of international popularity, however, its supply was most closely associated with market towns of Sarkhej near Ahmedabad and Biana, south-west of Agra. The dye is processed by way of an exacting technique which leaves little margin for error. Indigo itself is not soluble in water. To dye cloth, the precipitate from the immersed leaves of the indigo plant is mixed with an alkaline solution to create 'indigo white'. The cloth or yarn is then dipped in such a solution, and colours blue as the white indigo oxidizes on contact with the atmosphere. A repeated dipping into the vat darkens the blue colour. Although fast, the indican merely coats the surface of the fibres of the cloth; it therefore tends to rub off and is prone to leaching when washed.

Adjective dyes require a mordant for any degree of permanency. Mordants include the metallic salts of alum, chrome, iron and tin as well as salt, vinegar, caustic soda, slaked lime, urine and the compounds or solutions of certain leaves, fruits and wood ash. The Indian dyers are famous for their skilful use of alum and iron metallic salts that capture the elusive colours of red and black. Red is achieved by combining a source material of the colouring substance alizarin with alum, the results ranging from pink to deep red. By mixing an acidic solution of iron – often just rusty scrap – with tannin or jaggery, black dye is created. Such iron mordants have the unfortunate quality of biting rather too hard on natural fibres, thereby rotting the black of a woven or embroidered pattern.

Red dyeing with a mordant is complex. It is a wonder that the many chemical interactions required should have been developed at all, and that the secrets of the trade then not divulged to European interlopers until the seventeenth century. A crucial step in the mordanting procedure is the treatment of the yarn or cloth with an oily or fatty substance, and afterwards with an astringent such as lime. This prevents the subsequent addition of the mordant, alum, from drying on the cloth and crystallizing. The red colouring agent alizarin may then be added.

One of the common sources of alizarin lies within the dried root of the madder plant, *Rubia tinctoria*, and its relative *Rubia munjista*. In Sanskrit, the plant is known as 'madhur'. Of equal importance as sources of alizarin were the indigenous shrubs and trees of the *Morinda* genus, and the plant *Oldenlandia umbellata*. The dyestuff from the roots of the *Morinda citrifolia* and *M. coreia*, as well as *M. augustifolia*, *M. bracteata*, *M. tormentosa*, *M. umbellata* and *M. tinctoria*, is known as 'al', 'ach' and 'surangi'. *M. citrifolia* was formerly cultivated as a field crop on an extensive scale throughout India and the shrub dug up when three or four years old. The

'Toran' (doorway hanging)

colouring matter is found in the young root bark and mature tree roots are discarded as worthless. After chipping the roots, the free acids are removed by washing in water. A neutral morinda root solution, when well mordanted, has a dyeing power that excels that of the madder.

The root of *Oldenlandia umbellata* (commonly known as 'chay') was another significant dye source root-crop. Grown throughout the same region, the chay that was cultivated on calcic soils was found to yield a superior dye. The seashell-rich rivurine deltas such as the Kistna were therefore favoured for chay cultivation. The root of the growing plant absorbed the calcium which, after processing, added a bright and almost luminous quality to the red colour.

The well-known condiment turmeric, from the perennial herb *Curcuma longa*, has had its uses over the centuries as a fugitive yellow dye source. The rhizomes of the plant contain curcumin, a sharp yellow colouring agent that readily dissolves in water. Easy to use, but not durable, turmeric is used in combination with other more subtle dyes as a bright colour wash for such textiles as the memorable turbans of the north-west of India, and as a top coat of dye to create secondary colours such as green. Yellow colouring of a more permanent nature is achieved by mixing a boiled solution of the flowers of the myrobalan tree (of the *Combretaceae* family, akin to the myrtles) with mango tree bark and an alum solution to form a mordant. A semi-fast green colour is commonly obtained by coating blue dye with the myrobalan. The fruit of the myrobalan is a source of tannin.

The flowers of the hardy annual plant safflower, *Carthamus tinctorius*, enjoy a long history as a dyer's drug, both in the Subcontinent and further west, through the Middle East to Europe. The petals yield a fugitive yellow and, after treatment with alkalis, a fine ponceau colour especially suitable for silk.

Yarn

The most famous textile material associated with the Subcontinent is cotton. The export of fast-dyed cotton cloth to Europe revolutionized the garment and furnishing fashions, agricultural practices and the textile manufacturing industry of the seventeenth and eighteenth centuries. Silk from China and India was patterned and coloured within the Subcontinent as well, but it was the inexpensive, robust and washable Indian cotton cloth that transformed European social attitudes to attire, decoration and cleanliness.

Cotton has been cultivated within the Subcontinent for the manufacture of textiles since at least 1750 BC, the date ascribed to the Mohenjo-daro fragments of the Indus Valley. The perennial form of cotton plant is a slow-growing and warmth- and water-demanding shrub; its cultivation in more northerly climes was therefore limited. By the sixth or seventh century AD the more robust annual variety, *Gossypium herbaceum*, was grown in India, its cultivation spreading both westwards and to South-East Asia by the thirteenth century. The textile craftsmen of the Subcontinent have enjoyed, therefore, the considerable advantage of many hundreds of years experience in the cultivating, handling, processing, dyeing and weaving of cotton yarn.

Cotton fibres are harvested by collecting the hairy fruit of the plant, bush or tree. The seeds are separated from this fibrous boll by ginning, often with a hand mill, and the raw cotton disentangled by hand into bundles of usable fibres ready to be handspun by spindle or simple spinning wheel. The professional cotton carders of India use an instrument resembling an oversized violin bow to pluck at the mess of bolls and thus create a semblance of order and a light, as well as loose, mass of fibres. Cotton fibres are short stapled and must be spun together to create a continuous yarn of useful plying and weaving length. Throughout the Subcontinent is found the hand-powered floor spinning wheel, the 'charka', a development of the hand spindle. By teasing and twisting a leader of yarn from a bundle of cotton and knotting this on to a horizontally mounted spindle shaft, the spindle is turned by a connecting belt or string attached to the wooden wheel. By spinning the wheel, slowly at first, with the right hand, the fibres are fed to the spindle with the left, and the yarn collected on the spindle.

The supply of ready-bleached cotton yarn from the power mills of Bombay and Ahmedabad has all but supplanted the hand preparation of fibres throughout India. The spinning wheel is therefore mainly used to wind bobbins of different coloured yarn ready for handloom work.

The silk textiles of India are renowned for their exotic colours and fine patterning resulting from a complex series of dyeing and weaving processes. The double-ikat cloth from western India and the gold and silver brocaded scarves and saris from Varanasi are luxury commodities that delighted the nobility of the courts of Java and the Mughal Empire. Wild silk is indigenous to India and has been harvested from trees adjacent to the eastern river systems of the Subcontinent. Cultivated silk is found at higher altitudes, within the mulberry groves of the Indian hill districts. This domestic production would once have been overshadowed by the import of silk yarn from China. Silk supplies are now either indigenous, or purchased by way of Bombay merchants, originating from China, Japan, Korea or Italy.

Silk, unlike cotton, is an ideal fibre for textile manufacture. In its cultivated form it has length and elasticity, is strong and even in diameter, fine to the touch and takes dyestuffs of all types beautifully. The larvae of the wild silkmoth live on the leaves of oak and mulberry trees and pupate by secreting the gum sericin and a cocoon of very long silk fibre – often one kilometre or more in length. In the wild state the chrysalid leaves the cocoon after eight to ten days by dissolving the gum and eating its way through and out of the fine fibrous cell. Both actions damage the silk thread and the cut fibres must be carded and spun before use; this yarn is known as wild or spun silk. Cultivated silkworms, *Bombyx mori*, meet their death before they are ready to escape. At the end of the cocoon stage, the dormant larvae are dropped into a cauldron of boiling water, thereby preserving the entire length of the silk filament. Much of the sericin is dissolved by the boiling water and the remainder of the gum removed after the winding off of the lengthy filament or after the cloth-weaving process.

safflower
(Carthamus tinctorius)

madder
(Rubia tinctoria)

turmeric
(Curcuma longa)

indigo
(Indigofera tinctoria)

chay
(Oldenlandia umbellata)

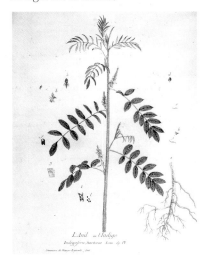

35

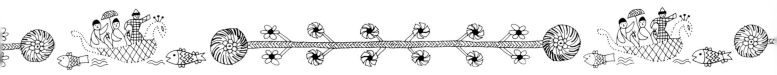

3   The Techniques of Textile Decoration

There are three main techniques of traditional textile decoration: loom-weaving and decorating; resist-dyed work, which includes tying and dyeing as well as painting and printing processes; and embroidery, which will be discussed in the next chapter. The skill of weaving and decorating cloth on the loom reached its zenith some two hundred years ago in the shawl workshops of the Vale of Kashmir, the backstreets of Varanasi and Ahmedabad – home and workplace to the weavers of lush gold and silver brocades – and within the muslin and jamdani factories of the Gangetic floodplains. Embroidered and printed trade cloths were the highly prized produce of the western state of Gujarat, and printed and painted export calicoes the hallmark of the Coromandel Coast. The finest white embroidery and pulled threadwork on white cotton, known as 'chikan', was found in Lucknow, Dacca and Calcutta, and delightfully embroidered and decorated quilted covers, 'kanthas', were a folk craft of Bengal and Bihar. In the western region of the Subcontinent, cotton and silk yarn and cloth was decorated for both the domestic and the South-East Asian markets by imaginative combinations of tying, dyeing and loom weaving.

For the most part, the regional pattern of decorated textile production exists today much as it was before the Industrial Revolution, despite changes, not always for the better, in the lives and skills of the workers. Certain techniques of textile preparation and decoration are now becoming rarer and less refined; the chikan work of Lucknow and the mashru weaving of central and western India are two such cases. Others – the double-ikat dyeing and weaving of Gujarat, for instance – are in danger of disappearing altogether – a result of the lack of inherited technical skills rather than of any decline in quality. There are some traditional techniques, however, such as the ikat production of Andhra Pradesh, that have been re-invigorated or adopted by other communities to flourish once more.

Loom-woven and Handwoven Textiles

Most of the weaves of India are weft faced; that is, the wefts are interlaced with the warps and beaten down to cover them entirely; some are warp faced, as is the mashru cloth; and others are a balance of warp and weft weave, such as the double-ikat work of Gujarat, Orissa and Andhra Pradesh. It is very much easier to interlace the warp and weft threads of a cloth if the warps are held in tension with a loom. Throughout the Subcontinent, traditional textiles are woven on horizontal, or low warp, looms that vary in technical advancement from the single-heddle, angled and frameless loom of the patola weavers of Patan to the semi-mechanized Jacquard looms of Varanasi.

In the past, the yarns used by weavers would have been exclusively handspun and of naturally dyed cotton or silk, but are now more likely to be machine-spun and of synthetically coloured cotton, rayon and silk. The dyed or undyed yarn is prepared for the loom by warping, a simple process that saves both time and materials. The prepared yarn may be wound off a roll or drum on to a frame that will keep the threads in the right order for 'dressing' the loom. In India the warps are stretched out over posts set on the wall or floor of a courtyard to a house or workshop, and are wound on to a wooden ground frame or spiralled on to a vertically rotating warping mill. Often the warps are held in place and tensioned on the loom by being wrapped over a rigid frame of wood with a winding mechanism to draw the finished cloth to the weaver on the breast beam – the brocade weavers of Varanasi and the ikat craftsmen of Orissa, for instance, use this type of loom structure. Alternatively, the warps are tensioned by way of a warp beam tied to a post; again, in Andhra Pradesh, the warps are looped directly round a post set in the ground. When the warps are 'fed' into the loom in this manner the excess bundle of yarn is strung from a beam on the ceiling. There is usually more than one loom to each room in a house or small workshop and the warps of one loom would often seem to the observer to intertwine and interlace with the other in a confusion of colour, cloth and apparatus.

Aside from the uniquely simple single heddle loom of the Patan patola weavers and the backstrap weaving of the tribal peoples of Assam and Orissa, the most common form of weaving apparatus in the Subcontinent is the relatively simple treadle loom. More often than not, this loom is laid on the ground and the peddles which the weaver operates are set in a pit; he sits on the ground with the cloth beam apparatus on low supports above his thighs. Such a construction is rigid, simple and strong and is often set outdoors in the cool of a shaded courtyard. From the plain white cotton khadi cloth to the single-ikat furnishing cloth of Andhra Pradesh, the bulk of the Subcontinent's fabrics are produced on the treadle loom and other developments of this semi-mechanized weaving apparatus, making it the mainstay of the Indian textile crafts industry.

Kashmir Shawl Weaving

The much-sought-after tapestry-woven Kashmir shawls of the eighteenth and nineteenth centuries were woven on very simple looms, despite the sophistication and complexity of production for foreign commissions. The merchants of the past, however, have now been replaced by tourists, and today the woollen shawl cloth is woven on continuous warped treadle looms, and is then embroidered by outworkers. The abundant variations in quality and style of the embroidered goods in, for example, Srinagar reflect a thriving craft industry catering for both the fancies of Western travellers and the traditional demand for shawls from a wider Indian domestic market.

Many-heddled Loom Weaving

Since the early decades of this century many of the simple pit treadle looms of India have been 'modernized' to increase the speed of production without, necessarily, any resultant decline in quality. Many looms have additional shafts and pattern rods operated by hand for the insertion of

supplementary wefts and, less commonly, supplementary warps. More often that not, a father and his son or daughter will work such a pitloom, the child inserting the supplementary wefts with a small bobbin of coloured or metal thread. In this manner the skills and traditions of handloom production become second nature to the young of a weaving family.

'Kalamkari' (penwork) panel of Vahara, the boar incarnation of Vishnu

Rarer and more complex are the cumbersome drawlooms requiring not only the weaver but also a 'drawboy' to manage extra leashes that are attached to the warps. More common are the dobby and Jacquard looms found in the traditional yet highly commercial handloom weaving centres such as Varanasi. These ungainly contraptions look less like handlooms and more like remotely controlled machines, for the leashes are manipulated by a set of levers mobilized either by a series of pegs or, as with a Jacquard loom, by a punched card. As the direction of the weaver's work travels from side to side of the growing fell, so the perforated card feeds through the machine setting the leashes in position for the next arrangement of warps to be opened or closed to allow the passage of the weft yarn within a shuttle.

Some of the most highly prized saris and cloth lengths are made of either heavy brocades of precious metals or, conversely, translucent muslins with ethereal and delicate floral patterning. Of the former, Varanasi is the most famous twentieth-century source, producing brocades known as 'kinkhab' (little dream); this manufacture is now commonly associated with wedding saris. The most famous of the fine and lightweight patterned cloth is 'jamdani', woven to the east in West Bengal and Bangladesh. There the looms used are simple and the pattern detailing labour-intensive, for true jamdani work requires a dextrous and delicate touch. Seated at the loom, the master and his assistant weave patterns with coloured or metal thread, once guided by tracings of the designs on paper laid under the warps, but now by lilting verbal instructions. The jamdani technique is essentially tapestry work, the wefts forming the pattern where needed, being threaded through the warps with a wooden needle. Such short lengths of weft threads are then extended to complete a design by being looped and tied around a warp. Each design or motif of weft-patterned work may have two or more joins, skilfully sewn and woven so as to be invisible. By using thread as fine as the compound weave, the weft patterns seem to merge and float within the cloth, rather than appear as an overlay of woven decoration.

Resist Dyeing

The resisting, 'screening' or 'covering' of pre-woven yarn or finished cloth with a removable yet impermeable substance is a common method of textile decoration in the Subcontinent. The placement of the dyestuffs in the resist technique can be controlled in various ways, but there are two main methods of regulating the patterning. Firstly there is the tie-and-dye technique, in which yarns or textiles are 'screened', or partly 'screened', by being tied with impermeable threads. The second creates patterns either by painting or printing with a substance that will react with the dye to fix the colour (mordant resist dyeing), or by applying an impermeable and removable substance such as mud, gum or wax, that will successfully resist the colour when the cloth is dipped into a dye bath, yet may be removed by dissolving, washing, or washing and heating.

Tie-and-dyed Ikat Textiles

Known throughout the world as 'ikat', a derivative of the Malay word 'mengikat', meaning 'to tie' or 'to bind', this technique entails binding (resisting) and dyeing the warps or wefts before weaving. Bundles of threads are meticulously arranged to a prepared design and bound with impermeable yarn or rubber bands so that as the yarn is dyed with a range of colours, the areas protected from each dye are resisted in succession. Within the Subcontinent the cloths produced by this yarn resist work are called 'tie-and-dye', 'bandha', 'patola', 'chitka' and 'telia rumal'.

The techniques, the quality and the originality of design of the ikat textiles of India are unsurpassed. Of special significance is the patola cloth. Patola weaving is an ancient Indian textile craft well known as a luxury export to Malaya and Indonesia in the sixteenth century, where the patola was cherished as the garb of the nobility and revered for its magical and sacred properties. Today these fabulous and costly silk textiles are only made in Patan, Gujarat, on a very limited scale.

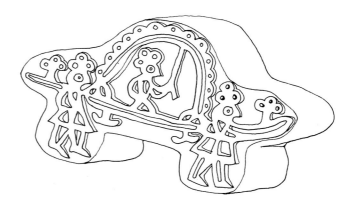

Carved woodblock for printing an embroidery pattern

Whereas the double-ikat weaving tradition of Gujarat is in danger of extinction, the weavers of Orissa and Andhra Pradesh have prospered, flooding the handloomed cloth market with fashionably coloured and patterned single- and double-ikat saris, garment and furnishing cloth.

The ikat textiles of Andhra and Orissa are woven and prepared with essentially the same technique as their illustrious forebears to the west, but the looms and tools are quite different. In Orissa the fine, detailed and curvilinear patterning is achieved by using very thin yarn, and by tying and dyeing small numbers of threads – commonly two or three (compared with twelve in Gujarati patola ikat) – in a cluster on a rectangular frame. Orissan ikats are woven on counterbalance flyshuttle treadle looms, the structure resting on the ground over the edge of the weaver's pit. The heddle and harness system hangs from the ceiling and the warps to be woven are either wound on to a cloth beam or run over a beam and tied in the roof space out of the way. In Andhra Pradesh the warps are tied ready for dyeing at their full length, whereas the wefts are tied in groups on a frame, fanning out to form the segment of a circle from a central peg. The simple pitloom is anchored in position by posts set firmly in the ground, and the warps stretch from the weaver across the room to focus and be wrapped around a post.

Detail of a patola double-ikat sari

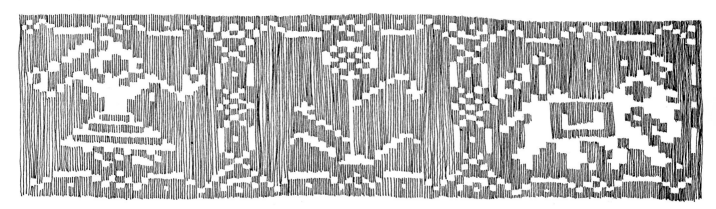

Printing and Painting

Aside from the direct application of pigment on to the surface of prepared cotton yardage, the techniques of fixing colour to woven cloth to create patterns and compositions again involves either the use of resist, mordant resist, or combinations of the two, applied with a pen, brush, metal or wooden block or through a stencil. In order to resist the dye, areas of the cloth that are to form the pattern or design are coated with impermeable substances such as wax, gum or rice paste, resin, starch or mud. Once the cloth has been dyed, the resist substances are removed by immersion in hot or cold water, or by ironing or brushing. Mordant-resist textile decoration techniques involve the painting or printing of dyestuffs that will react with mordant-prepared cloth; or alternatively, the painting or printing of mordants on to cloth which, when immersed in a colour bath, will cause the dyes to react and be fixed by the patterns of applied mordant.

Resist Application and Mordant Resist

Textiles patterned by the combination of these techniques are produced in most regions of India. Some of the finest examples are the strikingly finely printed 'odhnis' of Saurashtra and the equally colourful 'ajarakh' cloths of Sind, Kutch and western Rajasthan.

The traditional processes for the production of ajarakh cloth begin with the washing and bleaching of machine-loomed white cotton from Bombay or Ahmedabad. This is then softened with a mix of oil, carbonate of soda and fresh dung (which is a bleaching agent), and then dipped in a myrobalan solution. Using wooden blocks, resist paste of gum and lime is then stamped on to it to protect those areas to remain white. The resisting and mordanting pastes of iron acetate and alum mixed with gum and mud are applied with differing pattern blocks to protect and fix the black and red areas respectively.

Those areas stamped with the alum paste are then sprinkled with powdered clay and the whole cloth is left to dry in the sun. The textile is then dipped into an indigo vat for blue, and after a careful degumming, ensuring that the mordants are not smeared, boiled in an alizarin bath for red. Deeper shades of red are achieved by the application of resists and alum mordant as necessary and a further immersion in alizarin. Following a rinse and a wash in a solution of cow dung, soap and soda ash, the cloth is beaten and polished to enhance the blue sheen of the indigo dye. The finest ajarakh is printed, resisted and indigo dyed on both sides of the cloth.

The application of resists in combination with mordants is practised in the east of India at Masulipatnam in Andhra Pradesh. As with the cloth from Kalahasti to the south, the agents that control the patterning are traditionally applied with a 'kalam' (pen), and so the term 'kalamkari' (penwork) applies to production at both places. The kalam workers of Kalahasti are at pains to point out, however, that the Masulipatnam work is a less rigorous medium of textile decoration, as printing blocks and wax resists are used for most of the work rather than just the pen alone.

Many of the cloths for which Masulipatnam is renowned are still printed and painted in the traditional manner. Machine-loomed cotton cloth known as 'kora' is bleached by repeated immersion in a solution of goat or buffalo dung and frequent rinsing in the river or canal. The cloth is then mordanted in a myrobalan solution, to which is added fresh buffalo milk to prevent the spreading of the dye on application. Outline printing of floral, bird and animal patterns with black (made of iron salts and gum), with red (alum with gum), or with both colours, then follows, and the cloth is left to dry for two or three days. After washing, the cloth is scalded in a vat of alizarin and madder solution, enhancing and fixing the red patterning and removing the myrobalan and gum juice. Bleaching then takes place, leaving a white cloth patterned in red and black. Cleaning, bleaching and starching follows prior to the painting of the cloth with yellow and green colours. Yellow is achieved by boiling myrobalan flowers in water and by applying the solution with a simple kalam made from a short pointed bamboo stick whose dye reservoir is a felt pad bound with string. Pressure on the myrobalan-soaked pad allows the artist to control the release of the dyeing agent. The dyes are fixed permanently by dipping the cloth in an alum solution, after which it is part-bleached in cow dung solution to give the yellow an attractive clarity of colour. Finally, the cloth is washed and soaped.

The Coromandel coast of India was once a world-renowned source of fine hand-painted textiles; fortunately, its textile-producing traditions have survived in a newly invigorated form within the southern Andhra Pradesh temple town of Kalahasti. The painting of scenes from the Hindu epics on cotton cloth was revived by the establishment of a training school by the All India Handicrafts Board in 1958. This kalamkari craft industry is now thriving, supplying domestic and overseas markets with 'traditional' temple cloths.

Unlike the Masulipatnam kalamkari cloth, the hangings from Kalahasti are decorated entirely by freehand use of the kalam pen. Machine-loomed cotton cloth is washed to remove the starch and soaked in myrobalan solution ready to take the black dye. Once spread out on the ground or on a low wooden bench the cloth is ready to be sketched on by the artist. Outlines of figures and designs are first drawn freehand with charcoal sticks made of tamarind twigs. The subjects of the illustrations are either traditional, taken from Hindu epics, or such innovations as scenes from the Bible or even company logos. The kalam for fine linework is a pointed bamboo stick, six to eight inches long, swaddled at the sharpened end with felt or wool that is tied to the cane by a net of string. The felt pad holds the dyestuff, which may be released by slight variations of finger pressure to run down to the point of the kalam and on to the cloth as the designs are drawn. Black outlines are painted with the kalam using a solution of salts of iron. An alum solution is painted as infill with a bamboo kalam which has a flattened and softened brush-like end. The cloth is then immersed in a solution of pobbaku leaf, surudu root bark and manjishtha root and the mordanted areas are coloured red. Double mordanting of figures and patterns with alum creates tones of red and the cloth is then bleached in a solution of goat's dung. The final colours of yellow, blue and green are painted on the cloth as infill and detail with a kalam. Yellow is obtained by painting a myrobalan flower solution on areas pre-mordanted with alum, blue by applying indigo mixed with a little alum, and green by coating the yellow areas with indigo.

A young girl of the Meghwal caste tassel-making in Hodka village in Banni Kutch

Goat-hair belt (above) made using the split-ply method, from west Rajasthan; and (right) Ishwar Singh, of Jaisalmer, Rajasthan, preparing a split-ply camel girth of goat hair

'Chaklas' (square hangings): (left) made by the Rabari of Kutch; (centre) made by the Bharwad, or the Charan, Saurashtra; and (right) a Ganesh chakla made by the Ahir herders, Saurashtra

(Left) 'Dharaniyo' (cover for a pile of quilts), with floral designs and an embroidered border, made by the Ahir herders in Kutch. The central field is of 'roghan' work (the design is printed on with a mixture of thickened oil and pigment).

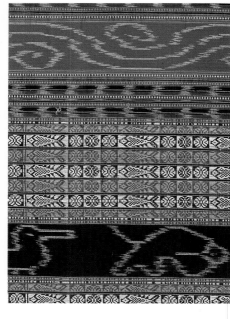

(Opposite) Double- and single-ikat cotton 'saktapar' sari, with detail of border (above). From Sambalpur District, Orissa.

Weaving, in Barpali, Orissa. (Top left) An elderly man preparing the loom heddles; the weaving of ikat saris on flyshuttle pitlooms (left); winding yarn on to a bobbin for weft work (bottom left); and (below) starching the warp with rice paste.

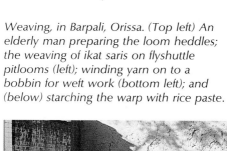

In Sanganer, Rajasthan, a young man carves a wooden printing-block for textile patterning

Woman block-printing yardage in Jodhpur, Rajasthan

Late nineteenth-century mural from a 'haveli' (mansion) in Nawalgarh, Rajasthan, depicting a block printer at work

(Opposite) Contemporary bedcover, decorated with 'kalam' (pen) work and printing, from Masulipatnam, Andhra Pradesh

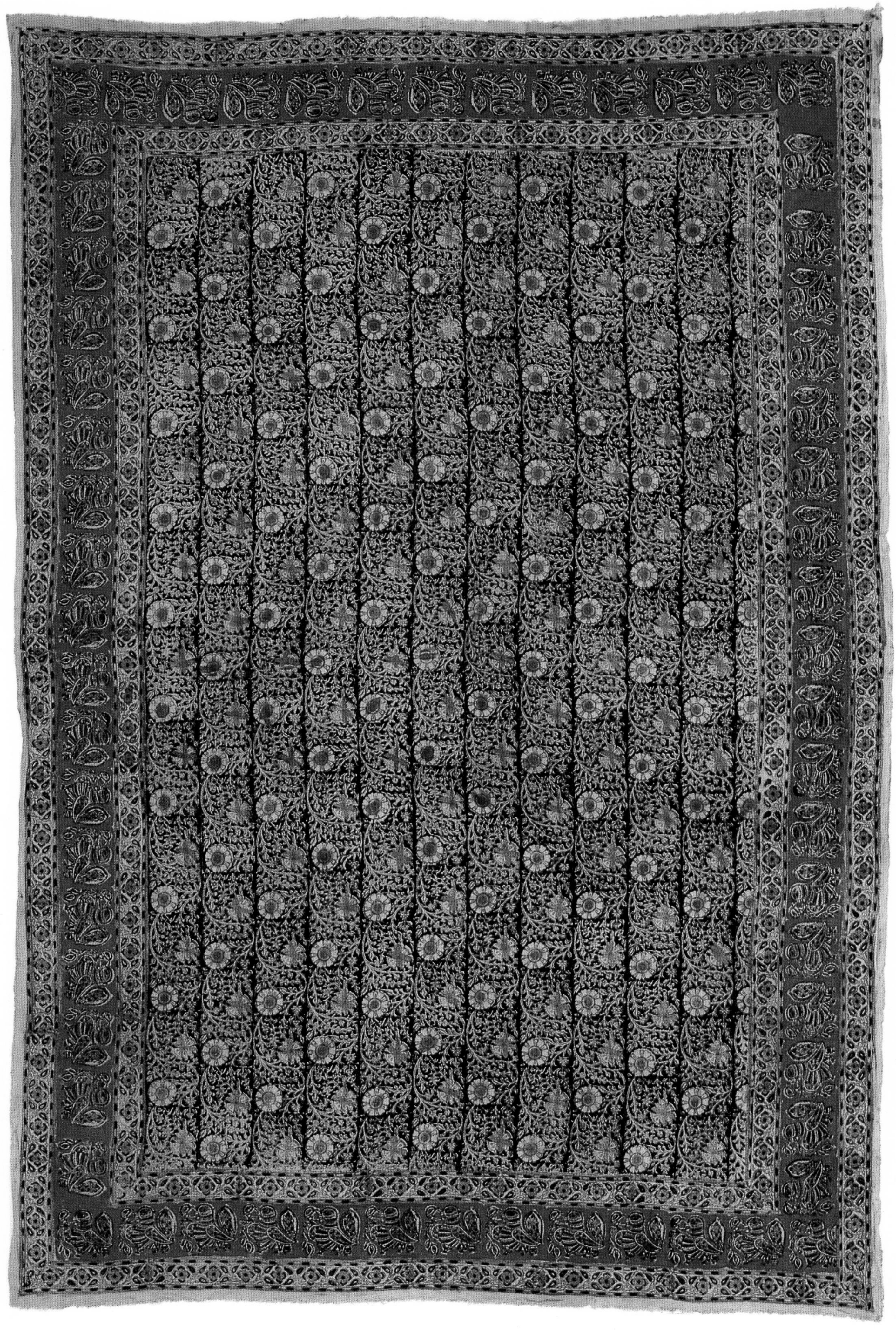

Printed cloth, drying after being washed in the pond at Barmer, Rajasthan

(Opposite) Detail of a grid-patterned sari (known as 'garchola'), made with 'bandhani' (tie-and-dye) work, in Mandvi, Kutch and finally dyed red in Jamnagar, Saurashtra

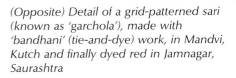

Silk bandhani 'odhni' (shawl), from Jamnagar, Saurashtra, made for the wedding of a Gujarati woman of a wealthy family

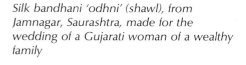

(Bottom left) Khatri dyer, from Mandvi, Kutch, squeezing excess dye out of the cloth during the tie-and-dye process

(Below) Freshly printed textiles being washed in the Sabarmati river, Ahmedabad, Gujarat

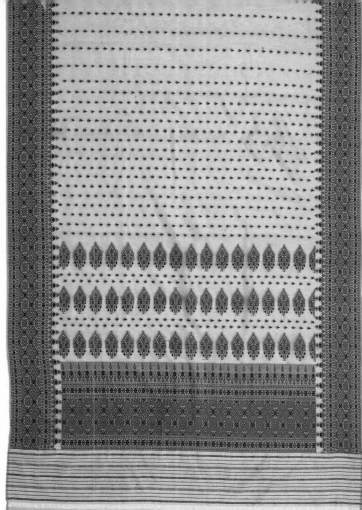

Sari woven in 'muga' (wild silk) in West Nowgaon District, Assam

(Top left) Weaving ikat saris on flyshuttle pitlooms, in Barpali, Orissa

(Opposite) 'Kinkhab' (silk and metal thread) 'gaghra' (skirt), woven in Jamnagar, worn by the Kathi women of Saurashtra

Workshop weaving of fine saris, using semi-automized Jacquard looms, in Varanasi

Late eighteenth-century 'rumal' (cover) depicting a marriage ceremony. Muslin, embroidered with coloured silks, from Chamba, in the Himalayan foothills.

(Top left) Khatri tie-and-dye workers in Mandvi, Kutch; (centre left) dyeing 'leheria' (wave pattern) turban cloth, in Jodhpur, Rajasthan, and (bottom left) preparing 'ajarakh' cloth with yellow dye, at Dhamadkha village in Kutch

(Right) Detail of contemporary 'kantha'- work embroidery, from Jamalpur, Bangladesh

Preparing the dye bath for the dyeing of 'ajarakh' cloth, in Barmer, Rajasthan

Khatri dyer of Kutch, binding cloth as part of the tie-and-dye process

(Opposite) Block-printed 'mata-ni-pachedi' shrine cloth made by members of the Vaghri caste in a street near the Central Post Office (below), in Ahmedabad, Gujarat

Section of cotton 'bandhani' (tie-and-dyed) 'odhni' (shawl), probably from Jamnagar, Saurashtra

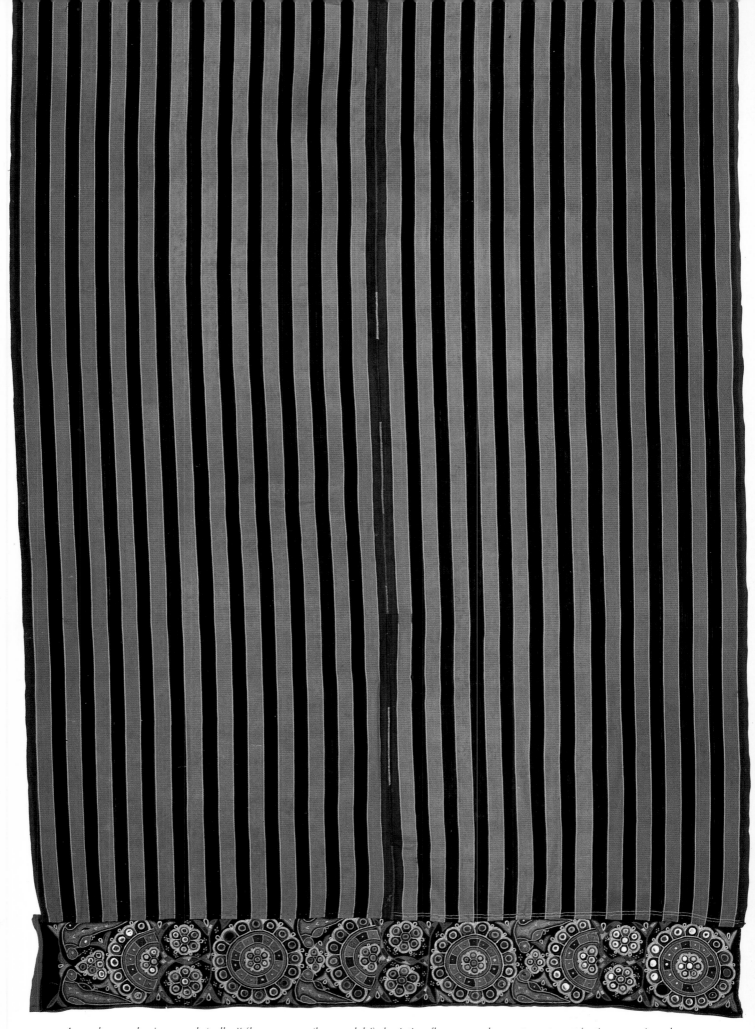

A mashru and mirrorwork 'odhni' (known as a 'karamulah') depicting flowers and parrots, worn at festive occasions by Ahir women of Kutch, Gujarat

4   The West

The prosperous state of Gujarat, the princely land of Rajasthan and the neighbouring province of Sind in Pakistan are predominantly arid regions where agriculture can flourish or fail according to the vagaries of the annual monsoon rains. This area has long been famous for the cultivation of cotton and indigo and for the early use of mordanted (therefore fast) dyestuffs; indeed the rivers themselves are legendary for their chemical properties, which were said to impart a special brightness to the colours obtained through the dyeing and mordanting process.

The terrain of western India is dramatic, but for most of the year there is visible only a landscape painted with shades of yellows and browns, broken by the irrigated fields of rich green and punctuated by clusters of thorn and other hardy trees adjacent to the wells and seasonal lakes. By way of relief to the monotony of these dull tones, the people of the region have a deep-seated need for colour which is vented in the vibrancy of their clothes, animal trappings and house decorations: the richness of the region's textile culture is indeed evident to the visitor as well as to the follower of fashion in the West. Most of the hand- and screen-printed yardage – the brightly coloured and patterned cotton that is used in the West for summer dress, blouse and skirt fabric – comes from Rajasthan. Recently, however, in London as in Delhi, there has been a proliferation of decorated handbags, small rucksacks and holdalls made up from embroidery pieces, and much of this ephemeral fashion market has been supplied from the dowries of Gujarati women.

Western India lies in close proximity to Iran, the Middle East, Afghanistan and Central Asia, and has strong cultural links with this largely Muslim world. Over the centuries, immigrants and invaders from these neighbouring lands have settled here, become assimilated and formed castes within the Indian social structure. Their influence on textile design and production techniques has been keenly felt, as both patrons and practitioners of the textile arts. The area has always been blessed with busy ports; Surat, Broach and Cambay were the most important in Mughal times; and other historic ports include Mandvi in Kutch and Tatta at the mouth of the Indus. Karachi (in Pakistan) and Bombay, the ports built by the British, and Kandla, a deep-water port in Kutch, serve the area today. In times past, all of these ports had access to important export markets including the Arabian Gulf, Yemen and the Arabian peninsula, through the Red Sea to Egypt, where Cairo was the entrepôt for goods in transit to Europe as well as to the coast of East Africa; southwards and eastwards the boats rounded Cape Cormorin and Ceylon to trade with Indonesia and on to China. Ocean sailing boats and coastal vessels have carried the textiles of western India to all points of the globe since prehistoric times. To the Greek and Roman Empires was sent cotton cloth, then to the Muslim world quantities of the cheap printed calicoes, and then, by the seventeenth century, to Europe the exquisite commercial embroideries and to South-East Asia the venerated double-ikat cloths.

Embroidery

Throughout the seventeenth century, Gujarat was probably the most important centre for fine commercial embroidery in the world. Today, the belt comprising Kutch and Saurashtra up through northern Gujarat to western Rajasthan and the Thar Parkar district of Sind in Pakistan is the world's richest source of folk embroidery. Marriage costumes, wall hangings, quilts, cradle cloths and animal trappings are embroidered, appliquéd, decorated with beadwork and embellished with mirrors, sequins, buttons and shells. Each caste passes on unchanged from generation to generation its own distinct designs, colours and range of stitches which, together with the cut of their garments and their own particular tie-and-dye and block-printed designs, form the major visual part of a caste's cultural identity.

Professional Embroidery

Mochi Embroidery   The Gujarati embroidery tradition was maintained for many years by the 'Mochi' embroiderers of Kutch and Saurashtra, who worked for the court and for the merchant and landowning castes. The Mochis were traditionally cobblers and leather-workers by trade, who developed the art of embroidering in fine silk chain stitch, using the 'ari'. This is a fine awl which has a notch incised just above its point to form a hook, and is akin to the European tambour hook. The thread is held below the cloth to be embroidered and the point of the ari is pushed through the fabric to pick up and pull through to the surface a loop of thread. The point of the ari is then again inserted into the fabric through this loop and the process repeated, so that a continuous line of chain stitch begins to be formed. The ari is an adaptation of the cobbler's awl and the Mochis would appear to have developed their methods of ari-work embroidery from the craft tradition in Sind of embroidering leather belts, shoes and bags. Until recently, the ari was being used for domestic embroidery by the Lohanas of Banni Kutch.

The embroidery silk was imported from Europe or China, and the satin embroidered on was again either imported or produced nearby, in Surat, Mandvi or Jamnagar. The centre for Mochi embroidery was Bhuj, the capital of Kutch, but some Mochis worked elsewhere in Kutch and others moved to Saurashtra to work for the Kathi landowners there. The Mochis produced ari work for 'gaghra' (skirt) pieces, 'cholis' (bodices), sari borders, children's caps, 'chaklas' (embroidered squares) and 'torans' (pennanted doorway friezes). They also embroidered the devotional pichhavai hangings for temples, illustrating the Lord Krishna, as manifested at Nathadwara, Rajasthan.

The motifs usually embroidered were 'buttis' (flowers derived from Persian or Mughal sources) often with parakeets perched on them. These were interspersed with figures of peacocks or 'putali' (women), sometimes both; or, more rarely, with caparisoned elephants and saddled horses. The heyday of Mochi embroidery was most probably the late nineteenth and early twentieth centuries, when Mochi embroiderers were practising in Kutch and in Saurashtra; but the courts were to lose their wealth and powers of patronage, as were the Kathi landowners, and many of the merchant families who had traditionally commissioned Mochi embroidery left for Bombay. By 1947, Mochi embroidery was virtually extinct.

Chinai Embroidery   In the nineteenth and early twentieth centuries, there was a community of Chinese embroiderers living in Surat, south Gujarat, who nevertheless produced work that was completely Chinese in both design and technique. Their embroidery was known as 'chinai' work and they made either garment pieces and shawls embroidered with fine floss silks, or saris, cholis, children's dresses and borders, precisely embroidered with tightly spun two-ply silk. Long narrow border strips with interconnecting motifs of birds and flowers, predominantly in white against a coloured silk background, were a favourite of the rich Parsee community, and many examples of this work can still be found in Bombay.

Domestic Embroidery

Kutch, Saurashtra, western Rajasthan and the adjoining province of Sind in Pakistan are areas of arid scrubland, some of which is cultivatable, but much of which affords only seasonal pasture for flocks and herds of sheep, cattle and camels. Thus the inhabitants are mainly small-holding farmers or pastoralists, with merchant and artisan communities in the towns. They are divided by caste which, as in the rest of India, is here usually equated with a hereditary occupation. These castes reflect a cultural diversity that has resulted from the influx of peoples over the centuries through both Iran and Central Asia. This in turn has had its bearing on the domestic embroidery tradition in western India.

The people living in this region share a common dowry tradition. In addition to the usual gifts of jewelry and household utensils, a bride will bring to her husband's home a large number of richly embroidered textiles which she and the women of her family have worked. This dowry will consist of costume for the bride and groom, hangings for her new home and trappings for their domestic animals, all intricately embroidered or appliquéd and often incorporating small mirrors. When the bride leaves her parents' home

Quilted 'khotrie' (dowry bag)

'Bukhani' (wedding shawl) border

and moves to that of her parents-in-law (where the groom continues to reside after marriage), she traditionally brings with her a set of hangings, usually wrapped in a large chakla. In Kutch and Saurashtra a 'toran' is hung above the doorway to the main room of the house, the pennants that hang down from it representing mango leaves, symbols of good luck and a welcoming device to gods and men alike. On each side of the doorway is hung an L-shaped textile known as a 'sankhia', and beside these are 'pantorans', smaller friezes and smaller chakla squares.

The display of embroidery takes pride of place at the great wedding celebrations and religious festivals, and on a more limited scale it brings colour to everyday life too. Distinctive embroidered clothes are worn as the proud badge of caste cultural identity, and indeed help to form that identity. Each caste has its own style of embroidery, range of colours and repertoire of stitches. Caste and social status is indicated by the colours and materials used. The merchant communities often work in silk, whereas the farming and pastoral castes usually use cotton or wool.

Costume in this part of India is embellished with embroidery and mirrorwork and made as colourful as possible in order to provide a pleasing contrast to the generally dun shades of the surrounding desert landscape. Particularly vivid are the clothes of the children and young women. The cut is full, to combine maximum protection from the hot sun with a good circulation of air to promote coolness. The designs and motifs used are handed down unchanged from generation to generation; they are inspired by the indigenous flora and fauna and local mythology. It is a tradition that has survived intact and remains alive due to relative geographical isolation and the absence of industrialization.

Aside from weddings, the most important events of the year are the great religious festivals held at places of pilgrimage all over Rajasthan, Gujarat and Sind. At these festivals caste members can meet, marriages are contracted or celebrated, and religious rites performed. Here the crowds are entertained by bards and musicians, and camels, horses and oxen are traded and raced. These animals are caparisoned with embroidered trappings – on their backs, necks, ears, legs, chests, muzzles and even on the oxen's horns. The patterned camel girths are woven out of goats' hair, the wooden saddles padded out with patchwork quilts; oxen are bedecked in embroidered or appliquéd covers called 'jhul'. Families traditionally travel to a festival on their camels, or else in ox-carts. The wooden carts are covered with an appliquéd tent known as a 'maffa', which provides shelter from the hot sun.

Styles of Domestic Embroidery
The Sindi Style　　This style is prevalent in the Thar Parkar and adjoining districts of Sind, in Banni Kutch and in the western Rajasthan districts of Barmer and Jaisalmer. Designs are abstract, or very formalized representations of flowers and foliage, worked in primary colours using mainly satin stitch. The most prolific practitioners of this style are the women of the Meghwal (or Meghwar), leather workers by profession and caste, who are centred on the Thar Parkar district of Sind, but may be found in Rajasthan, west of Jodphur and in Banni Kutch. Their most delightful work embellishes marriage cholis, purses and 'bukhanis' (wedding scarves). Their work is of two types: either profusely embroidered floral and disguised bird designs, mostly on a red ground, supplemented with mirrors and beaded pom-poms; or else couched metal threadwork on a black background. All the work in the Sindi style is characterized by a great range of fine stitchery

and vivacity of embellishment and colour-matching. Sadly, many of the women of the embroidering castes who would joyfully and lovingly produce such fine work for their own marriages have been drawn into the money economy and now produce shoddy embroidered piece-goods for the export market. Designs and colours are imposed from the commercial fashion and trading world and they no longer have the time to embroider in their own beautiful style. Other castes embroidering in the Sindi style are the Lohana and Memon merchant castes of Sind and Kutch, the Pali and Dars landowning castes of Sind, the Rabari shepherds of Sind, the Sutar carpenter castes of Sind and western Rajasthan and the Muslim herding castes of Sind, Banni Kutch and western Rajasthan.

The Kutchi Style   The Rabari shepherd, Kanbi farming and Ahir herding castes are the main practitioners of what can be loosely termed the 'Kutchi' style of embroidery, characterized by predominant chain and open-chain stitching and the profuse use of mirrors in the case of the Rabari and Ahir women. They embroider in white, yellow, green and red and sometimes a little blue, mainly in cotton on red, orange, white, black, or green cotton or satin. Motifs are floral with accompanying parrots or peacocks, although human and animal figures are represented with women dancing, churning butter or carrying water pots on their heads. The shisha, or abla, mirrors used are bought in either pre-cut rounds, or in large pieces to be cut up with scissors. Much of the mirrored glass was once only manufactured at Kapadvanj in Gujarat, but now it is also made at Bhuj in Kutch and Limri in Saurashtra. Other castes embroidering in the Kutchi style are the Rajputs and Oswal Banias of the Wagad tract of Kutch, the Mistri carpenters and at one time the Bhansali farmers of central Kutch.

Saurashtra Styles   The Saurashtra peninsula is home to three main styles of embroidery:

1 The Kathipa Style   Torans, chaklas, and other items of domestic embroidery are worked with 'heer' (floss) silk in elongated darn stitch which runs in both horizontal and vertical directions (in the manner of Punjabi phulkari work, giving the same textural variety). The elongated darn stitch is used in combination with herring-bone stitch. Designs are geometric with two crenellated

borders, the outer appliquéd and the inner embroidered surrounding either a chequerboard pattern, containing repeats of an eight-pointed star pattern, or a regular arrangement of diamonds and triangles. Mirrors are inset at regular intervals around the borders and at the interstices of the designs. The embroidery silk used is purple or red, with details figured in white, yellow or green, worked on an indigo blue, or sometimes white, cotton ground – a combination of colours that was set off well by the whitewashed walls on which the textiles were hung.

The first practitioners of this style were women of the Kathi landlord caste. About one hundred years ago, they turned away from embroidery to beadwork, and began to employ professional Mochi craftsmen to produce embroidery for them. The Mahajan or Bania merchant community around Bhavnagar imitated the Kathi style and most of the Kathipa work to be found today is their work.

The Kanbi farmers of Bhavnagar still work in the Kathipa style, embroidering torans, sankhia, pachhitpati, chaklas, chandarvo and pantorans. Kathi houses often contained a 'bhitiya', or 'besan', which could be a single large hanging but is usually a long embroidered frieze, from which hung a series of large chaklas. Frieze and chakla were attached each to the other by means of lozenge-shaped pieces of different coloured cloth, and the whole besan hung right along one wall for festive occasions.

2 The Figurative Work of Kanbi and Associated Farming Castes   The Ahir, Satwara, Mehr, and Aboti communities of north-west Saurashtra, the Boreecha of Morvi district and the Kadwa Kanbi and Lewa Kanbi of central and south Saurashtra are all prolific embroiderers. The patterns on their embroidered textiles depict naturalistic flowers, animals, birds and human figures, usually outlined in cotton in chain stitch and then filled in using herring-bone stitch in cotton, or sometimes in silk. The colours used are bright reds, greens, yellows, blues and browns, usually on a white, yellow or orange cotton ground. This light background goes well with the mud-coloured walls of these communities though some embroideries are worked on a red, purple or blue background.

3 Ganesh Hangings   Some of the most characteristic of all the folk embroideries of

Gujarat are the images of Ganesh (the elephant-headed god), embroidered on a white (and in the case of a 'Ganeshtapana', a pentagonal wall-hanging, often yellow) background. Ganesh is the remover of obstacles to happiness, and he is embroidered in the centre of the Ganeshtapana, often with his bowl of sweets and his companion rat, and almost always is set between his two wives, Siddhi and Buddhi. A border of flowers and birds, or else of animals, is worked around the edge of the Ganeshtapana.

The 'bari', a toran in the shape of an archway, has been popular over the last forty years. These are worked in herring-bone stitch, with some of the outlines in stem stitch, and are produced by the Kanbi of Kutch and most of the embroidering communities in Saurashtra (with the exception of the Kathis and the Rajputs). Ganesh resides in the centre of the arch and is flanked by figures of the gods, interspersed with flowers and bird and animal figures. Representations of pocket watches, bicycles, old British motorcars, and even gramophones are added, often seemingly at random. The embroidery designs used to be drawn out with a thin stick in black ink or soot by the best woman artist in the village. At a later date, special wooden printing blocks were made, and the design stamped out with a clay mixture made of broken roof tiles.

Most of the embroidered articles from Kutch, Saurashtra and western Rajasthan that are sold to the tourists on the streets of Delhi and Bombay come from the dowries of women who were married thirty or forty years ago. Since then, much has changed. Most women of the landowning and merchant communities gave up embroidery long ago. Today's women, of castes which in former times would have banished them to the seclusion of purdah, now spend their youth acquiring a fine education rather than trying to emulate the superlative embroidery of their grandmothers. Women are now exposed to the influences of television, radio, cinema, video and magazines; they no longer want to wear the sometimes heavy and cumbersome garments of their mothers' time and wish to fill their leisure hours with distractions other than embroidery.

Most pertinent to the decline of embroidery as a popular folk art, however, are two important factors: firstly, the introduction of education for girls, meaning that they now no longer have the time or the inclination to learn stitches from their mothers; and secondly, great upheavals in the caste structure over the last forty years, which have meant that many people now find work outside their traditional caste occupation. Consequently, in many areas, the need to keep up the appearance of caste identity through distinctive embroidered clothes and hangings has been superseded. Despite these changes, in areas where there has been little economic development – such as Kutch, north-west Saurashtra, western Rajasthan and the Thar Parkar district of Sind – people's lives have not undergone such radical change and the embroidery tradition remains strong, despite the threat of commercialization.

Appliqué

The appliqués of western India are generally large canopies and friezes used for celebrations or as animal trappings. Appliqué is both quicker and easier to work than embroidery and the articles are more hard-wearing. Appliqué in Gujarat is known as 'katab' (a word probably derived from the English 'cut-up') and usually takes the form of pieces of coloured fabric stitched on to a cotton ground. No examples of appliqué work survive from before the nineteenth century and it is thought that the technique was introduced into the area through trade contacts with either Europe or the Middle East.

The Kathis and their associated Muslim landowning caste, the Molesalaam, produced large friezes and canopies with dramatically drawn figurative work. Details of human and animal representations, filled in with old cotton and silk prints, mashru, bandhani, or patola cloth, greatly enhanced the charm of the textiles.

From the beginning of the twentieth century, the Mahajan merchants of Bhavnagar District produced many appliquéd textiles, applying mainly red cotton cloth to a white background. Designs of applied, highly stylized figures of birds and elephants were balanced by large areas of geometric 'dépliqué' work – where squares of red cloth were cut into and folded back, to reveal a pattern on the white background cloth of flowers, birds, or elephants set within foliage.

The Oswal Banias of western Rajasthan and the Wagad tract of Kutch made large wedding canopies in appliqué. They came in panels of six, nine, or twelve and more squares. Most of these squares are decorated by means of a 'snow-flake' pattern in white, applied to different coloured

backgrounds. The cloth for each snowflake is cut with the help of a cut and folded paper pattern. The Rajput, Satwara and other farming and herding communities also appliquéd chaklas, torans, chandarvo (canopies), dharaniyo (quilt covers). Some of the most interesting and practical appliqué textiles are the jhul (ox-covers) and maffa (ox-cart tents).

Beadwork

Beadwork is a needlework craft that was introduced into western India comparatively recently. In the nineteenth century, Bhattia and Bania traders from Kutch and Saurashtra were based in Zanzibar and were engaged in the trade with East Africa. One of the main items of trade with East Africa were Venetian Murano beads. Around 1850, these traders began to bring the beads into India. Of the beadwork articles that survive, the earliest datable examples were made by professional Mochi craftsmen, but by the turn of the century, Kathi women were taking to beadwork as a replacement for the craft of embroidery, which they now largely left to the professional embroiderers, the Mochis. The Mahajans, some of whose men would have been employed by the Kathi landowners, then also adopted the Kathi style of beadwork. The Kathi beadwork motifs portrayed divine and human figures, combined with flowers, cradles, racing camels, other animals and birds, and were worked in translucent and semi-translucent coloured beads set in a background of white opaque beads. Colours used in early examples were orange, yellow, green, purple and red.

The beadwork technique entails first of all making a border of beads for the whole textile, then attaching a thread to a top corner of the border. Three or more beads are then threaded on to a needle. The needle is then either taken through a bead of the border and pulled tight or over one of the threads of the border and back again through the last bead threaded on the needle. With even spacing, the process is repeated, until a row of looped beads hangs from the top border of the textile. On reaching the far top corner of the border, using the same process and working back in the opposite direction, beads are threaded on to the first row. The process is continued row by row, each row being attached at both the side borders until the bottom of the textile is reached. Different coloured beads can be worked in to form angular patterns.

63

Split-ply camel girth

'Bukhani' (wedding scarf) centre and end pieces

Split-Ply Camel Girths of Western Rajasthan

Perhaps the simplest form of textile structure found within the Subcontinent is that of the split-ply camel girths of Rajasthan. Worked by hand without a loom, these girths are stunningly simple, decorative and useful. The technique is also used to make camel necklaces and pot carriers. Until the advent of motor transport, life in the dramatic Thar desert region of western Rajasthan would have been insupportable without the domesticated camel. The whole of the Thar desert is the home to many thousands of these animals and they are used to pull carts, to draw water from wells, to plough the sandy fields, and as riding mounts and pack animals.

The men of the desert villages make the camels sturdy girths, sometimes out of cotton cord but more usually out of goat hair, using a unique technique. In his spare moments, the villager will take a bundle of specially prepared goat hair (either black or white) and with a simple spindle spin out yarn. The yarn is doubled to make it two-ply. Four-ply yarn is required for girth making, of which each ply is two-ply, and it is made by taking a length of two-ply yarn, folding it in four and then twisting it into a four-ply cord. The four-ply yarn may be either black or white, although one method of split-ply girth-making requires four-ply that is half black and half white, in which case two white two-plys are plied with two black two-plys. In every case, the final four-ply yarn is twisted very tightly as it will need to be much manipulated, twisted and untwisted. After twisting, the four-ply yarn is soaked in water and then stretched out in the sun to dry. This removes any kinks, opens up and thickens out the yarn, and sets the overtwist.

When dry, looped ends of the four-ply cord can be slipped on to a wooden stick or spindle. Ishwar Singh Bhatti of Jaisalmer — an expert camel-girth maker — uses fifty-two strands. Any more he considers difficult to work with. Taking adjacent elements, the ply of one cord is split open with the eye end of a large wooden needle and untwisted a quarter turn; the next cord is threaded through the eye and then pulled back through the first strand. This process is continued with adjacent elements all along the row and then worked down, row by row, with each individual cord reaching down and across the newly created fabric on a diagonal course ending at the selvedge. Turning down and across in the opposite direction the cord ultimately zig-zags down through the fabric from selvedge to selvedge. Patterning is dictated by the choice of the girth maker, who decides whether the cord is to split, or to be split by, the cord it meets coming along the opposite diagonal.

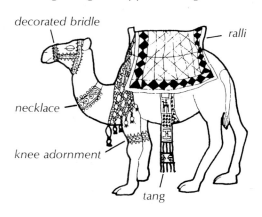

decorated bridle
ralli
necklace
knee adornment
tang

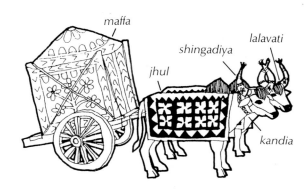

maffa
lalavati
shingadiya
jhul
kandia

Animal Trappings of Western Rajasthan and Gujarat

There are four basic pattern structures that can be formed using variations on this technique. The resulting girths can be monochromed (usually in black), have a black-and-white diagonally chequered pattern, or alternating black-and-white horizontal waves. The most interesting patterns are obtained with four-ply yarn that is half white, half black. Here the cord is untwisted in the cord-splitting process, so that two-plys of the same colour remain on the surface. The effect of using this refined technique on all the strands produces a diagonally interlaced layer in one colour lying on top of a diagonally interlaced layer of another colour. By restoring the twist to the cord, the colours can be counterchanged and the free floating layers linked together.

Appliquéd cotton 'ulech' (hanging) made and used by a farming caste, probably Ahir or Satwara, in Saurashtra

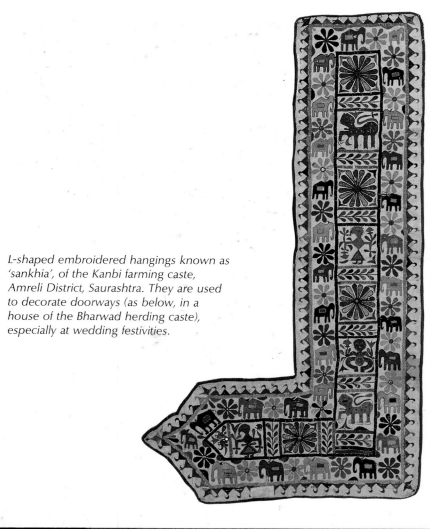

L-shaped embroidered hangings known as 'sankhia', of the Kanbi farming caste, Amreli District, Saurashtra. They are used to decorate doorways (as below, in a house of the Bharwad herding caste), especially at wedding festivities.

'Ralli' (quilt) of the Chauhan Rajput caste, Tando Mohammad Khan, Hyderabad District, Sind

'Jhul' (festival bullock cover) made of cotton, with flowers, wayside shrines, cows, women, peacocks, women churning butter with pots on their heads, deities on elephants, all embroidered in silk and cotton. Kanbi farming caste, Wadiya District, Saurashtra.

Pair of draught brahman bullocks caparisoned with matching embroidered jhul. Kanbi farming community, Bhimalad village, Saurashtra.

(Opposite) Wedding canopy of the Kathi landowning caste, Paliad District, Saurashtra

'Maan' (decorated room) of a Kathi house, with a swing-bed decorated with 'kinkhab' (silk and metal thread) brocade, near Lathi, Saurashtra

Wedding 'odhni' (shawl) of wool with cotton embroidery, from Barmer District, Rajasthan

Tie-and-dyed and embroidered cotton wedding shawl of the Memon merchant caste. From Diplo or Mithi, Sind

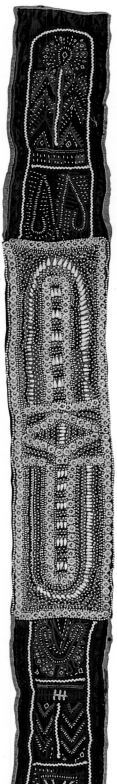

Cotton marriage blouse decorated with mirrorwork, tassels and silk and cotton embroidery. Made by women of the Meghwal leather-workers caste from Thar Parkar, Sind.

'Bukhanis' (wedding scarves), of the Rabari shepherd caste of Kutch; (far left) decorated with mirrorwork and embroidered with peacocks on a flowering bush, scorpions, women and water pots; (left) decorated with bead- and button-work, and with embroidery depicting abstract representations of elephants and peacocks on wayside shrines. Worn by the bridegroom.

(Opposite) 'Chakla' (square hanging) embroidered in 'heer' (floss) silk on cotton in the Kathipa style. Mahajan merchant caste, Saurashtra

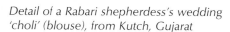

Detail of a Rabari shepherdess's wedding 'choli' (blouse), from Kutch, Gujarat

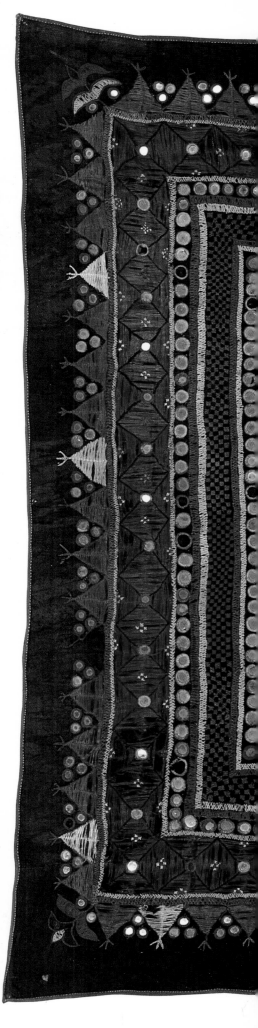

'Pabuji' (hero scroll), painted in Bhilwara, Rajasthan

'Bhopa' (storyteller) of the Nayak caste performing the Pabuji epic in front of a par scroll at Marwar junction, Rajasthan

'Pichhavai' (painted shrine cloth) from
Nathadwara, Rajasthan

'Ras mandal' wedding canopy (depicting the dance of Krishna and the gopis) at a Kanbi farming caste wedding, Bhimalad village, Saurashtra

Embroidered and mirrorwork 'torans' (friezes to be hung above the doorway to the most important room of the house), 'pantorans' (hangings) and 'khotrie' (bags) decorating the inner doorway to an Ahir herding caste home, Ratnal village, Kutch

(a) Bead- and button-work tobacco pouch worn by a Rabari shepherd bridegroom in Kutch. (b) 'Pachhitpati' (embroidered frieze to be hung above a doorway or beneath a shelf), embroidered with wool on cotton. Rabari shepherd or Charan farming caste, Saurashtra. (c) Festival trousers of a Rabari shepherd boy, Kutch. (d) Appliquéd and embroidered toran of the Vanya merchants, Bhavnagar District, Saurashtra. (e) Toran decorated with mirrorwork and embroidered with flowers, suns and birds. Ahir herding caste, Kutch. (f) Pantoran worked with an 'ari' hook by a professional embroiderer of the Mochi cobbler caste from Kutch. (g) Cotton toran with textured silk embroidered flowers on its pennants. Kanbi farming caste, Bhavnagar District, Saurashtra. (h) A 'kinkhab' patchwork fan of the Kathi landowner caste of Saurashtra. (i) Tobacco pouch of the Sutar carpenter caste, from Thar Parkar, Sind.

Shawl border, embroidered by a female relative and presented to a Kutchi woman of the Kanbi farming caste after she has successfully completed one year of marriage

'Bukhani' (wedding scarf), decorated with flowers, parrots and women turning into flowers, and embellished with mirrorwork. Ahir herders, Kutch.

Bharwad herder bridegroom and father with embroidered 'keriya' (jacket) and waistcoat; over the courtyard door is a toran (borrowed from a neighbouring Kanbi farming family), Bhimalad village, Saurashtra.

Appliquéd 'toran' (frieze hanging), with images of Ganesh and elephants, probably of the Satwara or Rajput castes, Saurashtra

(Below) Appliqué and mirrorwork chakla, Oswal Bania caste, Wagad tract of Kutch, or western Rajasthan

(Above) Beadwork 'chakla' (square hanging) worked in Venetian Murano beads to form designs of bushes, parrots, monkeys, cows and with a border of multiple images of women churning butter. Kathi landowning caste, Saurashtra.

'Ghughi' (horse's neck-cover) of the Kathi caste, Saurashtra

'Ganesh' doorway hanging of the Kanbi farmers, Saurashtra

(Opposite, above) Ganesh doorway hanging of the Kanbi farming caste of Saurashtra, illustrating the pantheon of the Hindu deities; and (below) Rabari shepherd boy wearing an embroidered 'keriya' (jacket) and printed turban, with a cotton shawl draped over his shoulder, in Anjar town, Kutch

'Ganeshtapana' – an embroidered shrine cloth used on special occasions by the Kanbi farming caste of Saurashtra

'Chakla' (square hanging) made with manufactured Indian beads. Kathi landowning caste, Saurashtra.

Overleaf:
(Left) Appliquéd 'ulech' (hanging) of the Kathi caste from Paliad District, Saurashtra

(Right) 'Dharaniyo' (cover for a pile of quilts) decorated with appliqué, mirrorwork, and tassels by the Rabari shepherds, Kutch. The embroidery depicts Ambadevi the mother goddess, seated on a horse or elephant; parrots, monkeys and peacocks; bushes and flowers; Srivan carrying his aged parents on a yoke; and a deity in a horse-drawn cart.

'Gaghra' (skirt), with cotton and silk embroidery and mirrorwork on cotton. Kanbi farming caste, Kutch.

Women of a Rabari shepherd family waiting for transport out of Anjar, Kutch, wearing 'bandhani' (tie-and-dyed) woollen shawls, embroidered 'cholis' (blouses) and gaghras of cotton, wool and synthetic materials

'Chakla' (square hanging), probably of the
Ahir, Saurashtra

Detail of a gaghra, showing silk
embroidery and mirrorwork on silk,
probably made by the Bhansali caste,
Kutch

Mashru gaghra of the Ahir, from Kutch

Embroidered front for a 'kurta' (smock), of the Sayeed community, Sind

'Guj' (wedding coat) of a woman of the Lohana merchant caste from Thano Bula Khan, Sind

(Right) Silk wedding 'aba' (dress) with silk embroidery, of the Memon merchant caste, Abrasar District, Kutch

Rabari father in the traditional 'keriya' (jacket) with hand-embroidered yoke, with his child, in Kutch

(Opposite) Rabari shepherd girl, wearing a 'choli' (blouse) of mashru weave with mirrorwork embroidery and a printed cotton skirt, at a religious fair in Kutch

Child's festival jacket, made by the Ahir of Kutch

Detail of a patola sari, decorated with a 'pan bhat' (pipal leaf) pattern, most probably from Patan, Gujarat

Block Printing

The Gujarat region was one of the great textile-exporting areas of India. Textile patterns were usually applied by block printing, and evidence of Gujarat's block-printed wares have been excavated at Fostat, near Cairo, the oldest of which have been dated as fifteenth century or earlier. These textile fragments are resist printed with unsophisticated yet pleasing designs typical of the hand-printed textiles of the region today. Then, as now, a resist substance was used on rather coarsely woven cloth (unlike the tradition of south-east India which uses a wax resist, on finely woven cloth). This method favours a fairly bold depiction of pattern. The most important centres for block printing are Sanganer, Jaipur, Bagru and Barmer in Rajasthan, and Anjar, Deesa, Ahmedabad, Jetpur, Rajkot, Porbandar and Bhavnagar in Gujarat.

Hand-printed textiles in Gujarat and the surrounding states of Sind, Rajasthan and Madhya Pradesh are made by Hindu and Muslim Khatris. Many of these Khatris claim that their ancestors left the Sind region after its conquest by the Arabs in the eighth century AD. Today, block-printed textiles fill a niche left by the mechanized mill textiles industry that dominates the cotton yardage production of the Subcontinent. Many types of hand-woven textiles disappeared, due to the competition from imported and domestically produced mill-made cloth during the last quarter of the nineteenth century. But there remained mainly localized demand for the block-printed, usually unstitched garments, such as dhotis, lungis, saris, rumals, pugris and jajam floor spreads; such a handmade commercial production has continued to find a ready market in Gujarat and Rajasthan, for the different rural castes have a preference for hand-crafted textiles for their own particular costumes.

In Gujarat and western Rajasthan, there are three main types of hand-printed textiles:

1   Ajarakh, worn by Muslims, is thought to have originated from Sind and is wholly geometric in patterning. Ajarakh cloth is block-printed on one or both sides. The name is most probably derived from 'azrak', the Arabic word for 'blue' – certainly indigo blue is the predominant colouring for these cloths. Ajarakh cloth is used as marriage wear by Muslim males. The Hindus in western Rajasthan and the Thar Parkar district of Sind wear a similarly patterned cloth in predominantly red colours called a 'malir'. Ajarakh is produced in Sind at Khavda and Dhamadkha, in Kutch, and at Barmer, in Rajasthan.

2   The Ahmedabad-produced screen-printed and block-printed designs of floral sprays and simulated bandhani on a predominantly red background.

3   The floral prints, with Persian associations, made at Deesa, in northern Gujarat, and in the Barmer and Jaisalmer regions of western Rajasthan.

All three types are printed against a background that is usually red, indigo blue or violet.

The Mughal-inspired floral prints of Bagru and Sanganer come from a different court-influenced tradition. Bagru and Sanganer are both close to Jaipur, the capital city of Rajasthan and though both now produce much block-printed cloth for the export fashion trade, they originally produced textiles for the local market. Sanganer fabrics were, on balance, more sophisticated; Bagru products were aimed mostly at local, rural women, but designs in both places reflected the Persian influence so prevalent in Rajasthan that dates back to the seventeenth century. Bagru prints are usually on a light brown background whereas Sanganer prints have a white background. In recent years Bagru has been more adventurous in its choice of block-printed designs, whereas Sanganer has turned in no small part to screen-printing.

In western India, cloth-printing blocks are usually made out of teak or 'sisum'. Blocks made at Pethapur, near Ahmedabad, are considered to be the best, and other block-carving centres are Farrukhabad, Mathura, Delhi and Jaipur. Poorer village block printers will use second-hand wooden blocks bought from their richer counterparts in the towns. Production in the larger towns is usually in the hands of the 'seths', the merchants who specify the kind of textile to be made, provide all the materials, printing blocks, dyes and fabrics, and contract out the work at piece rates to craftsmen specializing in each of the different operations required. In general, synthetic dyes have replaced some natural dyes, but the resists and ways of applying them and the sequence of dyeing operations all remain as labour-intensive as ever.

Printed and Painted Textiles

Mata-Ni-Pachedi

The Vaghris were once a wandering caste, some of whom have now settled in Ahmedabad, the great industrialized city of Gujarat. They make their living outside their houses, in a little lane by the Central Post Office, block printing and painting shrine cloths, which are known as 'mata-ni-pachedi' or 'mata-no-chandarvo'. Traditionally, the shrine cloths are made for ritual use by members of castes such as sweepers, leather workers, farm labourers, or by the Vaghris themselves. The shrine cloths always have as a central feature an image of the 'mata' – the mother goddess in her fearsome aspect – sitting on her throne, or mounted on an animal, brandishing in her hands the weapons needed to kill demons.

When any of the mata's devotees suffers illness or misfortune, he goes to the mata's shrine and vows that he will make a sacrifice to her if she will relieve him of his trouble. If his wish is granted, he pays for the shrine to be cleaned and decorated, and an enclosure made up of 'pachedi' (rectangular shrine cloths) is erected around the shrine, with the chandarvo, the great square shrine canopy, draped above it. A ceremony of chants and a trance-inducing dance is conducted by a priest-shaman, known as a 'bhuvo'. This is followed by the ritual sacrifice: the cooking and eating of a young goat. There is always a depiction of a bhuvo-priest, leading a sacrificial animal to the mata, on a pachedi, or chandarvo.

Before the decoration of these cloths can begin, the material must first be freed of starch and then bleached by a process that involves soaking it in a mixture of camel dung and water, then after washing and drying in the sun, soaking it again, this time in a mixture of salt and cow dung and then boiling. Next, it is immersed in water containing caustic soda and castor oil, and then dried. Once it has been dipped in a water-based solution of myrobalan and castor oil and dried, it is ready for printing. The motifs of the mata-no-chandarvo are then printed on with large wooden blocks, using a dye made out of rusted iron which has been soaked for a week in sugar solution thickened with a flour of tamarind seeds. This reacts with the myrobalan mordant to produce black. Most of the spaces between the black printed figures are painted with alum and starch using a chewed tooth-stick. The shrine cloths are then passed to Muslim dyers, who dye them in vats of alizarin, which reacts with alum to form a deep red.

Pabuji Par

The Pabuji par is a long pigment-painted cloth which depicts the epic story associated with the legendary fourteenth-century Rajasthani figure of Pabuji. Pars are used throughout most of Rajasthan by itinerant story-tellers (bhopas) of the Nayak caste. The par is used as a backdrop for a night-time recitation of Pabuji's heroic deeds. The par is stretched out in the open between two bamboo poles and the bhopa and his wife recite the epic story, accompanied by music from a stringed instrument called the 'ravanhattha'. It is a very complicated story, with many plots and subplots, and it is actually impossible to tell the whole story in a single night. The audience – Pabuji's devotees – are largely rural villagers. The core of the story is that Pabuji asks the Charan lady Deval (who is a living goddess) for the magical mare Kesar Kalami, which he is granted. After defeating Mirza Khan at Patan in Gujarat, and being rescued from drowning in Pushkar Lake, by Gogo Chauhan, the snake god, Pabuji goes to Lanka to steal Ravana's she-camels. In the process, he kills Ravana and on the way home he passes through Umarkot in Sind, and there the Sodhi princess Phulvanti falls in love with him. A proposal of marriage is sent to Pabuji, and is accepted.

On his way back to Umarkot, with his wedding procession, Pabuji is stopped by the Charan lady Deval, who tells him that his enemy Jindrav Khici is coming to steal her cows. Pabuji continues, but half-way through the wedding ceremony he is called away. Pabuji returns home to Kolu and then is persuaded to set out and recapture the cattle. He succeeds, but is later killed by Jindrav Khici, with Pabuji's own sword. Phulvanti then commits suttee, and ascends straight to heaven.

The Pabuji par cloths are made by members of the Joshi branch of the Chippa printing community. The cotton fabric ground of the cloth is first prepared for decoration with rice starch and then burnished with a heavy stone. The cloth is then divided vertically by three painted lines, and the outlines of the figures are drawn out in pale yellow. Gum-based gouache colours are painted on, starting with the lightest. Quite often the figures do not quite match the original outlines, but these will in any case be edged in black in a final stage in the process. Traditionally, the Chippas are supposed to paint in Pabuji's eye last. Once this has been done, Pabuji is considered to reside in the par, which is then ready for ritual use. There is always a little box for written information, painted by Pabuji's head. The painter's name, the place and date, the bhopa's name and the price he paid for it are all put in. This can be wiped out if the par is sold to another bhopa. In the past, pars would end their days by being immersed in the holy lake of Pushkar, near Ajmer.

Other pigment-painted textiles are found in Rajasthan at Nathadwara. Known as 'pichhavai', these temple hangings are used by the Vallabhacharya sect and depict Lord Krishna, manifested as Shri Nathji.

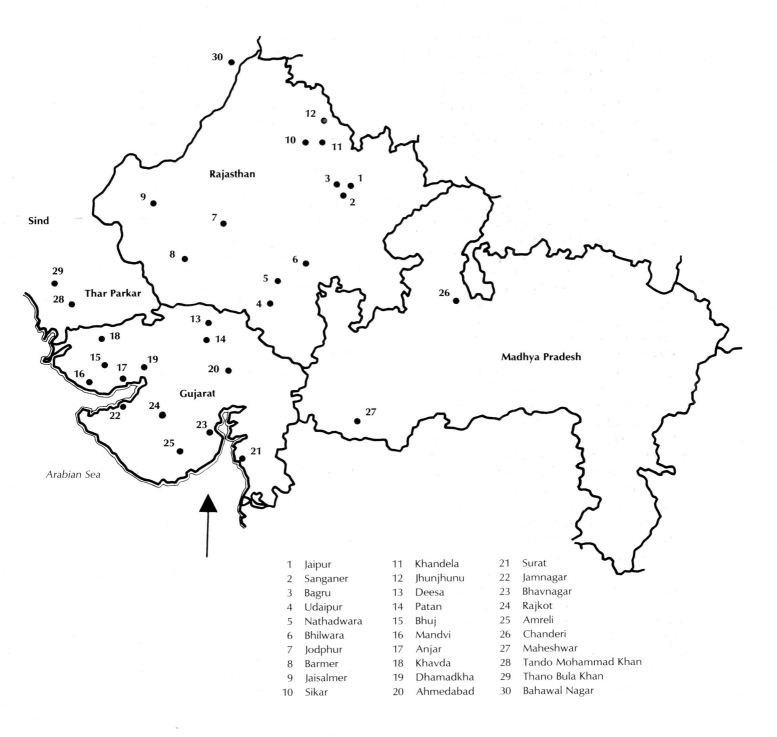

1	Jaipur	11	Khandela	21	Surat
2	Sanganer	12	Jhunjhunu	22	Jamnagar
3	Bagru	13	Deesa	23	Bhavnagar
4	Udaipur	14	Patan	24	Rajkot
5	Nathadwara	15	Bhuj	25	Amreli
6	Bhilwara	16	Mandvi	26	Chanderi
7	Jodphur	17	Anjar	27	Maheshwar
8	Barmer	18	Khavda	28	Tando Mohammad Khan
9	Jaisalmer	19	Dhamadkha	29	Thano Bula Khan
10	Sikar	20	Ahmedabad	30	Bahawal Nagar

Roghan Work

'Roghan' is a thick, bright paste which is used to decorate inexpensive textiles. Oil of safflower, castor or linseed, is boiled for a miminum of twelve hours and then poured into cold water, thus forming a thick residue. This is then mixed with chalk, coloured pigment and a binding agent. The sticky roghan mixture is then applied to the cloth, with a short stick or metal rod, which is twisted in the hand to get the roghan to come off the stick and on to the cloth. Roghan can also be block printed on the fabric using metal-faced blocks.

Roghan work is now only done at Nirona village in the Nakatrana Taluka of Kutch, where cloth decorated using this method is used as skirt lengths and for wall hangings. Formerly it was produced at Chowbari in eastern Kutch and at Ahmedabad, Baroda and Patan. In Ahmedabad, where skirt and sari borders were a speciality, roghan was painted on one strip, then another plain strip was pressed on top. These were left to dry in the sun and then peeled apart, leaving a coloured pattern on both strips. When roghan has been dusted with metallic powder it is known as 'tinsel work'. After a cloth has been painted or block printed, it is left to dry in the shade. When dry, it is gradually moistened with water, till the roghan softens. Gold or silver powder is then sprinkled on. Printing in this manner is done at Jaipur, Sanganer, Udaipur, Mandasor, Nasik, Ahmedabad, Baroda and Bombay, as well as at several centres in Madras and Andhra Pradesh.

Tie-and-dye Work

Bandhani

'Bandhana' and 'bandha' are Sanskrit words meaning 'to tie' (and it is from this Indian word that the English name for a spotted handkerchief, 'bandanna', derives), but this tie-and-dye technique is internationally known by its Malay–Indonesian name, 'plangi'. The term 'bandhani' refers both to the technique and to the finished cloth. By pinching up and resist tying areas of the fabric before dyeing, circular designs may be produced. Rajasthan and Gujarat are famed for their production of fine and prolific bandhani. Coarser bandhani is worked in Sind and Madhya Pradesh. The traditional garb of the rural women of western India includes the odhni shawl, made with the bandhani method. These shawls are of striking, swirling yellow or white dots, set in stylized floral patterns against a bright red or deep red ground. As part of the traditional set of choli, gaghra and odhni, the bandhani odhni looks stunningly colourful.

When simply tied, bandhani textiles are inexpensive and this is one of the cheapest ways for women of the poorer communities to dress in a colourful fashion. When tied with many fine knots, the price of bandhani rises steeply and is then the preserve of the richer classes. In Gujarat very fine bandhani odhnis tied on silk or fine quality cotton are worn as wedding garments by the women of the richer communities of merchants, landlords and the higher class of craftsmen. A bandhani sari that is traditionally worn for Gujarati weddings, and one that has become increasingly popular, is the 'garchola'. This is patterned with a gridwork of small bandhani squares of yellow dots against a bright red background, with motifs of lotus flowers, dancing women and elephants. The centres for this fine work, as well as for much of the simpler work, are in Kutch and Saurashtra.

Bhuj is a town with a great many bandhani workers, and in Abdasa Taluka and at Anjar, too, bandhani textiles are made; but it is in the beautiful old coastal port of Mandvi that some of the finest bandhani in India is tied. Kutchi bandhani patterns and colours tend to be more traditional, as they still have a local market to serve, though most Kutchi bandhani is commissioned by the merchants of Jamnagar, where it is often taken for the final dyeing process which adds red to the colours of the cloth. The water around Jamnagar is reputed to bring out the brightest red.

The largest bandhani workshops are in Saurashtra, especially at Jamnagar, though bandhani is also made at Porbandar, Morvi, Rajkot, and at Wadwhan, near Surendranagar. Simpler bandhani is made around Ahmedabad at Pethapur and at Deesa, in north Gujarat. All these towns have good river water available for dyeing and rinsing. The craft of bandhani is practised at many places in Rajasthan, but the finest bandhani is tied at Bikaner, and in Sikar district. In Rajasthan, a greater number of colours is used than in Gujarat and a lot of the colours are spot dyed by hand, rather than by being submerged in a dye-bath.

The tying of bandhani textiles is mostly carried out within the home, mainly by women or young girls. The material used is thin mill-made cloth, either a loosely woven silk known as 'georgette', or a cotton known as 'mal-mal'. The white, generally unbleached cloth is folded into four or more layers before the tying commences. The traditional technique of laying out the pattern – in pins or nails set in a wooden block, upon which dampened cloth is placed and then pinched up between the nails with thumb and forefinger – has long fallen into disuse. Two methods are currently employed, the first using wholly traditional materials. A 'rangara' (colourer) first marks off the fields with a cord dipped in a fugitive mixture, which in Kutch is known as 'geru'. This is usually a water-based solution of ruddle (red ochre) but can be of burnt sienna, or even soot. Then he stamps out with geru-coated wooden printing blocks the individual patterns. Any gaps in this printed pattern are made good by tracing over with a bamboo split.

A much faster and more precise method has become increasingly popular: a thin sheet of stiff, clear plastic is pierced with pin-holes forming the desired pattern. The sheet is then placed over the fabric to be tied and a sponge or rag dipped in geru is then washed over the sheet, leaving an imprint of the desired pattern on the cloth.

Once the pattern has been transferred to the cloth, the tying and dyeing can be undertaken in five stages:

1 With the fabric lying loose on the lap, the pattern is tied with plain cotton yarn. The material is pushed up from underneath with the long, pointed nail of the little finger of the left hand (or if this finger-nail is broken, a spiked metal ring is used). The knob of protruding cloth is then very rapidly tied round six to eight times and the thread led on, uncut, to tie up the next knob, and so on until all the dots to be left white are tied. These ties will act as a resist when the fabric is dyed, and upon untying will leave a pattern of little white rings, each with a tiny centre coloured by the last dye to be applied. (The fabric is always dyed with the lightest colours first.)

2 After the initial tying, the cloth is usually dyed with yellow or, very occasionally, another light colour.

3 Once it has been rinsed, squeezed and dried the cloth is tied again in the pattern that is to appear as yellow dots, and then dyed in darker colours such as green or red.

4 If other still darker colours – black, brown or dark red – are required, the cloth is tied again in the pattern that will appear as green or red dots. The parts of the cloth that are not to be dyed by the darkest colours are wrapped tightly in plastic, to stop them from absorbing the dye.

5 After the last dyeing processes have been completed, the cloth is washed and, if necessary, starched.

It should be noted that spots of colour can also be applied by hand, or by dip-dyeing at different stages of the process. This technique is used a good deal in Rajasthan, but only sparingly in Gujarat. Light colours can be applied after the cloth has been dyed yellow and before it is tied for the application of the next darker colour. Alternatively, at the end of the dyeing processes, particular white and yellow dots can be untied and spots of a darker colour, like blue, can be applied.

The finished cloth of two or three bright colours, against a dark background, is sold with its ties still intact. This shows that it is a genuine bandhani and not a printed imitation.

Leheria

In the nineteenth and early twentieth centuries, the Marwaris, merchants of Rajasthan and dominant business community of India, wore as their distinguishing mark elaborately tied, brightly coloured striped turbans. These turbans were made by the leheria technique ('leheria' in Hindi literally means 'waves'), and this process continues to be practised in the dyeing quarters of the Rajasthani towns of Jodphur, Jaipur, Udaipur and Nathadwara.

Leheria is a method of resist dyeing whereby material is rolled up and tied tightly at intervals, then dyed, so that the sections that have been tied remain undyed and the untied portions take the colour of the dye bath. Colour must penetrate right through the tightly rolled cloth, so the leheria technique can only be applied to highly permeable, thin, loose cottons or silks. Fabrics – generally turbans or sari lengths – are rolled diagonally from one corner to the opposite selvedge, and then tied at the required intervals.

The pattern results in diagonal stripes. If multicoloured stripes are required, they can be obtained after the first dye-bath by opening up some sections of the rolled fabric, leaving other sections still tied and tying up fresh sections, then dyeing the whole, or part, of the fabric in a fresh colour. After the patterning process has been completed in one direction, striping in the opposite direction can be added. First, the fabric is unrolled and then rolled up again from the next corner along. The dyeing and tying process is repeated and a chequered pattern of intersecting diagonals results.

Leheria is tied wet, with the fabric looped around a short, vertical wooden pole. The tying is arduous work, done by Muslim craftsworkers, and as with bandhani, leheria is sold with its ties still in place to show that it is the genuine article. A small end portion is unravelled to display the pattern.

Mashru

Mashru cloth is one of the most visually simple and striking of all Indian textiles. It has a shiny, satiny surface and is usually striped in pattern and woven in bright colours. Mashru is a warp-faced textile, made with a silk warp (now usually artificial silk) and a cotton weft. It has a satin weave that makes the cotton weft lie almost invisibly beneath the surface of the fabric. In Arabic, 'mashru' means 'permitted'. According to Islamic tradition, orthodox Muslim men were forbidden to wear silk next to the skin. But if mashru fabric was worn, although the surface of the fabric was of silk, cotton lay next to the skin, and as such the fabric was allowed by religious law. Mashru fabrics are also referred to by the term 'misru', which is derived from the Sanskrit word for 'mixed'.

A distinguishing feature of pre-twentieth-century mashru was the way in which sections of the warp threads were resist dyed and then, when untied and laid out on the loom, pulled and manipulated till they formed wave or arrowhead patterns. Very few modern mashru fabrics have tie-and-dyed designs, but are woven so that patterned stripes, running the length of the warp, are interspersed with plain coloured stripes. During the nineteenth century, there were many centres of mashru production, both in the north – mainly in Gujarat, Rajasthan, Agra and Varanasi – and in the south, at Hyderabad, Tiruchirappali, Mysore and Madras. It is now concentrated

between Bhuj and Mandvi in Kutch, at Patan in north Gujarat and also at Ajamgadh in Uttar Pradesh.

Mashru was a traditional export item, and was at one time sent to the Middle East in large quantities. In India, however, it is now no longer worn by rich Muslims but is produced to specific patterns mainly for Hindu villagers, in Gujarat, Rajasthan and Madhya Pradesh. It is used as material for blouses, skirts and pyjamas, and to edge garments and pieces of embroidery.

Patola

The products of the patola loom are predominantly sari lengths, which are among the most famous textiles in the world. These double-ikat textiles were woven in Patan, Surat and other centres, but there are now only two families of Jains weaving them in Patan. Cheaper patola imitations are woven in single ikat at Rajkot, Saurashtra, and in both single and double ikat in Andhra Pradesh in the south.

Within Gujarat and some adjacent areas, the richer Hindu, Jain and Muslim communities each had their own preferred patterns. Motifs were of flowers and jewels, elephants, birds and dancing women, used either around the border or in the central field, and always interspersed with geometric elements. Muslim communities, as would be expected, restricted themselves to abstract designs. All the communities who patronized the patola were wealthy (a patola sari now costs between 15,000 and 30,000 rupees); it was never a fabric the common man could afford. Indeed, patola was valued for its purity, because it was made of silk and, in addition to that, the weavers were of high caste.

The influence of patola was not restricted to India. Probably before, and certainly during the period of the European domination of Asia's sea routes, patola cloth was exported to the Indonesian archipelago, where it was used for ritual and court wear. Some of the very finest patola work, with many of the most striking designs, were sent to Indonesia. Fine patola in the 'vagh-na-kunjar' (elephant-and-tiger) design were particularly popular. Much of this export patola, however, was of a coarser and looser weave than that made for the home market.

Although the loom of the patola weaver looks simple, the methods of yarn preparation, weaving and adjustments to the woven cloth are labour-intensive in the extreme, requiring patience and

'Rumal' (cover)

hard-won skills. The silk used can be either imported or home-produced, and in its undyed state must be counted out, thread by thread, and collected in bundles. Each bundle is then tied and dyed to the particular pattern desired for each section of the patola cloth. These bundles are then untied, retied and dyed in the next colour needed for the design. The process is repeated until all the primary and mixed shades have been dyed into the yarn. The bundles are then untied and the warp threads carefully laid out in the proper colour sequence so that the pattern becomes visible when stretched on a frame. The weft threads, again observing the correct colour sequence, are wound on bobbins.

Weaving then commences on a very simple, horizontal handloom, with two string heddle bars raised with a lever, and a shuttle made of bamboo. Patola is always woven in plainweave. The weaving process aims to juxtapose accurately warps and wefts of the same colour in the design required. To this end, two weavers (known as 'salvis') work at the loom, which is tilted about thirty degrees from the horizontal plane to allow more light to fall on the loom and facilitate the constant readjustments to the weft threads. Such adjustments are done with a pointed metal rod the size of a pencil and, together with shuttle changes, dictate a slow pace of patola weaving – the fell advances at the rate of six to ten inches per day, which means that a sari takes nearly a month to weave. It is no wonder that such time-consuming and intensive workmanship may all too soon be a craft of the past.

Brocade Weaving

The Gujarat region is generally considered the home of silk and brocade weaving in India. Until recent times, Ahmedabad, Surat, Jamnagar and other towns in Gujarat produced 'kinkhab' brocade. Motifs, small in scale, of flowers, animals, birds and human figures were set out in regular horizontal rows, against a purple, red or green background. This Gujarati kinkhab was used for furnishing cloth or as skirt lengths. The other important weaving centres are Paithan and Aurangabad in Maharashtra, and Maheshwar and Chanderi in Madhya Pradesh. Paithani saris are famous for their brocade 'pallavs', which were woven with a weft of gold thread. The saris of Chanderi, near Gwalior in Madhya Pradesh, with silk warps and cotton wefts, have stylistic similarities to those of Paithan, whereas those of Maheshwar, in south-west Madhya Pradesh, traditionally have a chequered field with reversible borders, so that the border pattern is the same on both faces of the cloth.

Surat's Zari Industry

Surat is a once-famous port, situated in south Gujarat, north of Bombay. Three centuries ago, it was one of the biggest cities in India and the chief port of the Mughal Empire. At Surat is produced nearly all India's zari metal thread for brocading and embroidery, and the thin silver wire used for weaving.

The traditional method of manufacture involves the fusing of a covering of real gold on to a solid silver bar in a furnace. Then the metal is drawn through a series of dies of ever decreasing diameter, until thread of the fineness of human hair is obtained. This wire, by now a few miles long, will still retain a covering of fused gold. It is then beaten flat and wrapped around a silk thread.

In Mughal times, before Bombay superseded it as the main west-coast port, Surat was the premier port for the Haj pilgrims on their way to Mecca. These pilgrims provided the market for zari-work weaves and embroidery. The zari industry declined in the nineteenth century, due to competition from French machine-made zari thread, and only revived after the industry was given tariff protection in the 1920s. From then on, Surat maintained a stranglehold over the Indian market. Although it lost some of its main markets in Pakistan in 1947, it has recovered through partial mechanization and the introduction of artificial zari thread, where copper wire is silver-gilded by electrolysis.

As we have seen, western India is a prolific area for the production of a great range of textiles. Climatically it is blessed with ideal conditions for growing cotton, and is traversed by slow-moving rivers which, except at monsoon times, are well suited to the washing of textiles necessary between dyeing operations, and whose exposed areas of parched riverbed can be used for the drying of cloth. Gujarat is very much the textile lynchpin of the area, from whence skills of weaving, brocading, block printing, bandhani work and ikating seem to have spread out to adjoining areas and the rest of India. Gujarat's geographical position provided easy access to the inland market trade, and from its long coastline Gujarati merchants set out to trade in textiles with the Arab world, South-East Asia, Indonesia and China.

The rural peoples of western India comprise many castes. Caste identity is still very strong and distinctive textiles are worn as a mark of this identity. The diversity and quality of textile crafts is maintained because of the continued strength of traditional demand, with its vast variety of distinct localized preferences.

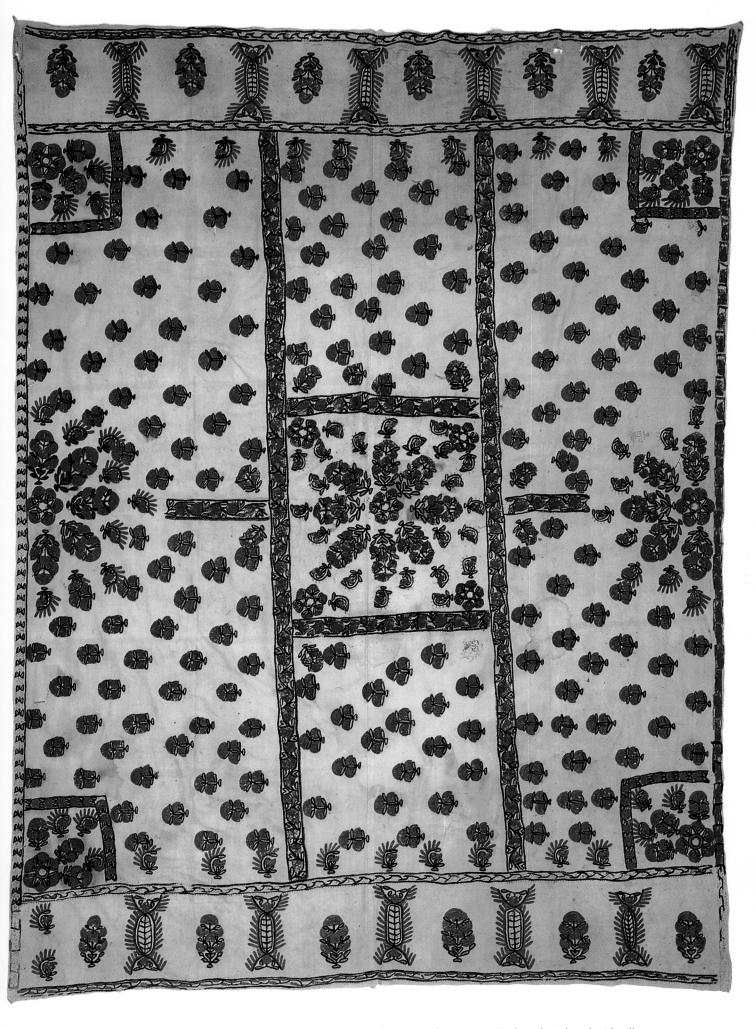

'Abocchnai' (wedding shawl) of the Dars landowning caste or Lohana merchant caste, Sind, embroidered with silk on cotton

Rabari shepherd boy, wearing an embroidered 'keriya' (jacket) and satin scarf, with his sister in Anjar town, Kutch

(Opposite) Patola decorated in the 'vohra-gaji-bhat' pattern, used by the Vohra Muslim merchant caste, woven at Surat, or Patan, Gujarat

'Toran' (frieze hanging) of the Kanbi farming caste from Amreli District, Saurashtra

Doorway of an Ahir house with an embroidered 'khotrie' (bag) hung from a post. Ratnal village, Kutch.

Panel of embroidered 'sankhtoran' hanging with mashru and brocade pennants, embroidered by Kathi women in Saurashtra.

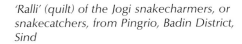

'Ralli' (quilt) of the Jogi snakecharmers, or snakecatchers, from Pingrio, Badin District, Sind

Interior of an Ahir herding caste house with embroidered mirrorwork 'dharaniyo' (cover for a pile of quilts), in Ratnal, Kutch

'Chakla' (square hanging) of the Rajput of Saurashtra

Appliquéd 'chakla' made by Kathi women of Paliad District, Saurashtra

Nineteenth-century patola silk double-ikat sari in the 'vagh-na-kunjar' (elephant-and-tiger) design, intended for export to Indonesia. From Gujarat.

Camels carrying textiles, Jaisalmer, Rajasthan

Muslim women wearing bandhani 'odhnis' and 'gaghras' (shawls and skirts), in Jaisalmer, Rajasthan

(Opposite) Block-printed cotton 'sadlo', a woman's wrap worn over a 'choli' (blouse) and petticoat in the manner of a sari, from Mandvi or Anjar, Kutch

Statues of 'Jakh' (deities mounted on horses) draped with Ahir herding caste embroidered 'torans' (frieze hangings), in Bhuj, Kutch. The Jakhs were legendary horsemen who freed Kutch from the rule of tyrants in the 10th century AD.

Roadside deity draped with a tie-and-dyed 'odhni' (shawl)

Woman's wedding shawl with couched metal threadwork, of the Memon merchant caste, Diplo District, Sind

Rabari shepherd families dressed to go to Gokul Ashteme (Krishna's birthday festival) outside Anjar, Kutch

'Gaudli' (embroidered mat used during marriage rituals), from Saurashtra

(Opposite) Groom's block-printed wedding shawl known as 'malir', which has been embroidered by the bride. Meghwal leather-workers caste, Barmer, Rajasthan

Detail of an 'ajarakh' backing cloth for a quilt, from Tando Muhammad Khan, Sind

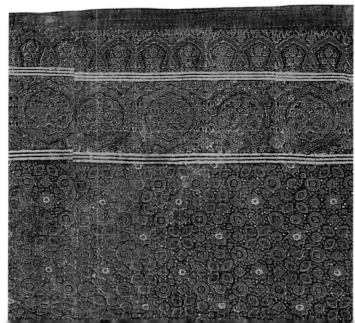

Woman carrying 'bandhani' (tie-and-dyed) cloth, in Barmer,
Rajasthan

(Right) 'Chakla' (square hanging) of the Kanbi caste from Saurashtra,
depicting two embroidered images of Lakshmi

Detail of a silk bodice sleeve embroidered in silk by the
professional 'Mochi' 'ari' workers of Kutch

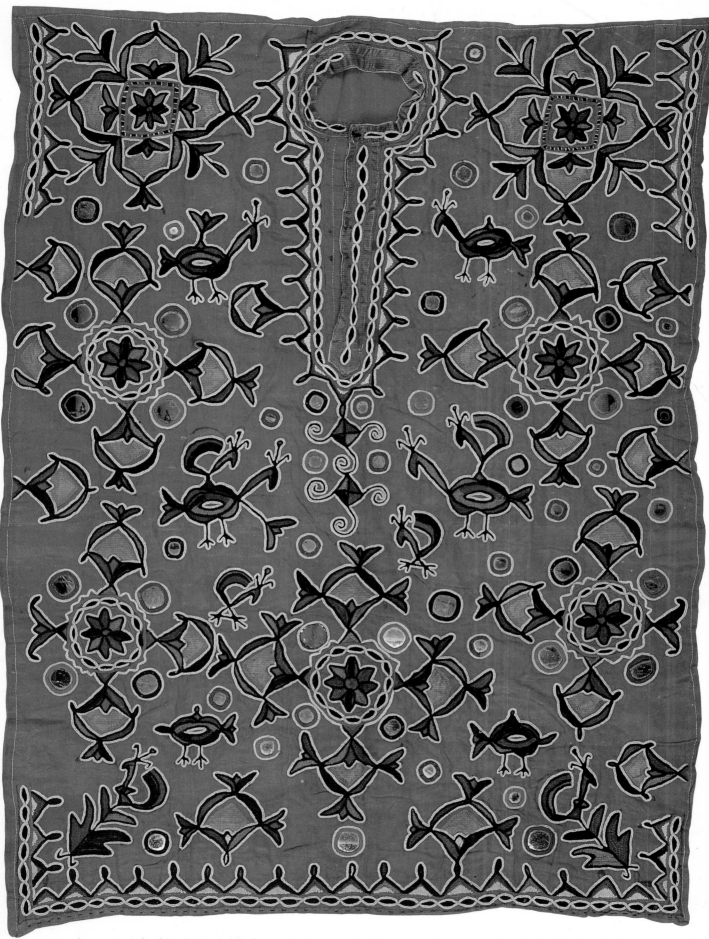

Front of a marriage bodice detailed with flowers and peacocks. Lohana merchant caste, Thar Parkar District, Sind.

(Opposite) Detail of an embroidered 'choli' (blouse) showing a woman smoking a hookah. Bhansali or Rajput caste, from Kutch.

(Overleaf) Fragment of a late nineteenth-century 'chikan'-work 'kurta' (bodice). A few large leaves or flowers of pulledwork are set in a background of tiny raised petals and leaves.

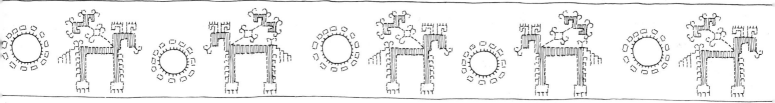

5　The North

Northern India is a land of great geographical contrasts. The Punjab, 'the land of the five rivers', and Haryana to the south-east, are both areas of fertile plains nourished by the waters and alluvium from the Himalayas. To the north of the Punjab, the hill states of Jammu and Kashmir and Himachal Pradesh nestle amidst the foothills of the great mountain range. For travellers and visiting officials, whether of Mughal or British

Colonial extraction, these hills were a haven of cooling breezes and memorable alpine scenery that offered an escape from the unremitting and unhealthy heat of the plains in summer. Returning to the plains and looking east beyond the ever-sprawling suburbs of Delhi, the vast and populous state of Uttar Pradesh runs from the soaring Himalayas to follow the holy river Ganges on its southward and eastward path towards the sea.

The Punjab and Haryana

The rich agricultural states of Punjab and Haryana are famous for the 'phulkari' (flower work) shawls that, worn with a tight-fitting choli and gaghra, formed the traditional costume of rural women of this region. It was a costume both spectacular and eminently practical. Phulkaris were made for everyday wear. Usually the border and field of the shawl were not so densely embroidered, with much of the ground cloth exposed. For ceremonial occasions, however, a special kind of phulkari known as a 'bagh' (garden) was made, in which the whole of the ground was covered with embroidery, so that the base cloth was not visible at all. On the birth of a baby, the grandmother, after a ceremony of prayers and distribution of sweets to the baby's aunts, would start to embroider a bagh. It would take several years to complete and was embroidered with special care to be used later at the grandchild's wedding, after which it would be kept as a family treasure.

Phulkari work was both a labour of love and a social occasion. The female members of a family would gather in the leisure hours of the afternoon to spin with the charka wheel and embroider, although it was usual for a phulkari to be worked by one woman alone to maintain a uniformity of stitches. Phulkaris were made for family use, or as gifts; very rarely were they made for sale. Young girls would learn stitches and designs from their mothers and grandmothers and would then start

to stitch a phulkari that they would later wear themselves. Motifs of flowers, birds and human figures were embroidered in soft untwisted floss silk (called 'pat' in Punjabi) in combinations of gold, yellow, white, orange or red, on a ground that was usually a brick-red colour, but could sometimes be black or white. The design was embroidered from the reverse side using darning stitch over counted threads. Only one thread was taken up with each pick of the needle, leaving a long stitch below to form the pattern. Stitching ran in both horizontal and vertical directions in order to give a variation in texture. It is easy to imagine the effect the light, playing upon the smooth sheen of the embroidered surface, would have on these juxtaposed sections of contrasting stitchery. In addition to darning stitch, double running stitch or chain stitch is used to form the outline of figures of birds, animals and humans, which are then filled in with darning or satin stitch. Satin or stem stitch is used on phulkari borders and blanket stitch or buttonhole stitch for finishing off the edges.

Although designs on phulkaris were often figurative, baghs almost always bore geometric patterning. In west Punjab the pattern, in the form of parallel lines or squares, was generally outlined in green thread before the bagh was embroidered. The work was of high quality and its geometric forms reflected the surrounding predominantly Muslim environment. Motifs and scenes from daily life — houses, temples, flowers, animals, wedding rituals and processions — are all represented in work from east Punjab, a colourful and lively display which made up for any lack of technical sophistication in design. All over Punjab and Haryana motifs used were drawn from nature. Images of vegetables and flowers, wheat and barley stalks, the sun, the moon, trees and rivers, Mughal gardens, kites and even playing-cards were stitched on phulkaris and baghs.

The embroidery was worked in silk thread from Kashmir, Afghanistan or Bengal, although the best quality silk was Chinese. Once dyed, at Dera Ghazi Khan (now in Pakistan), Amritsar or Jammu, the yarn was worked on a coarse handwoven cloth known as 'khaddar', which was produced in the villages by the 'jullaha' (the village weaver) in narrow widths of about seventeen to twenty-three inches. Two or three of these pieces would be joined together to form a phulkari. Khaddar was locally available, cheap, hard-wearing and most importantly, it was preferred to mill-made cloth, as its coarse weave facilitated the counting of threads necessary for phulkari work. It could

also be embroidered without a frame, as it did not pucker or pull.

Two other types of shawl should be mentioned. One is the 'chope', which is presented to the new bride by her maternal grandmother. It is embroidered in straight two-sided line stitch, so that the patterning is identical on both sides of the cloth. The other is a type of bagh, embroidered in east Punjab, called 'darshan dwar', which was presented to temples on the fulfilment of a wish. The two outer panels of a darshan dwar are embroidered with a row of large, tall gates, each with a triangular top. The central band consists of human figures, animals, birds and flowers. Trains, peacocks, parrots, wedding jewelry and pictorial scenes from village life can also feature as favourite motifs.

The embroidering of baghs and phulkaris virtually ceased about forty years ago, after the turmoil and mass upheavals of partition in 1947. Hindus and Sikhs were forced to migrate from west to east Punjab and Muslims (who included the majority of the khaddar weavers) fled from east to west; the khaddar cloth thus became scarce. This forced migration, along with post-

1 Srinagar
2 Leh
3 Jammu
4 Hissar
5 Delhi
6 Bhatinda
7 Lucknow
8 Tanda
9 Varanasi
10 Chamba
11 Lahore

Independence industrialization, meant that many rural people moved to the cities. In the villages as well, some aspects of agriculture were mechanized and rural life generally became busier. Women were now educated, and were subjected to the influences of the modern media, which meant that they were no longer inclined to spend their leisure hours embroidering. All of these factors have played their part in the death of a fine rural art. Attempts to revive the phulkari arts in Patiala and Chandigarh in east Punjab have failed because of irrevocable changes in the rural milieu. Similar attempts in Pakistani, west Punjab, have also met with little success.

Jammu and Kashmir

Jammu and Kashmir State comprises Jammu Province, the Vale of Kashmir and Ladakh. Jammu Province is a sub-montane area, bounded by the Ravi river to the east and the Jhelum to the west, and is bisected by the Chenab. To the north of Jammu lies the Pir Panjal range of mountains which separate the beautiful wooded and fertile vale of Kashmir from the rest of India. Kashmir is itself connected to the east by a series of high passes to Ladakh.

Jammu lies in the foothills of the Himalayas, with easy communications to neighbouring Punjab and Himachal Pradesh, and its textile tradition has much in common with that of neighbouring states. Phulkaris similar in composition and technique to those of Punjab were made in Jammu, as were rumals, in the Chamba style. The most notable textile products of Jammu Province are still the block-printed calicoes of Samba, a village about thirty miles south of Jammu where the hand-printing of textiles is a very long-established industry. Indeed, Samba is reputed to have been a centre of textile production long before many other famous Indian textile towns. Vegetable dyeing on handwoven cotton sheets was once the norm, with 'sonehri' (gold) and 'rupehri' (silver) printing a speciality, but now aniline dyes are used on mill-made cloth. Designs are most probably Persian in origin, with motifs of flowers and arabesques often in reds and greens on a yellow background. Animals, flowers and insects as well as human figures are also part of the contemporary printing repertoire, with bedspreads, tablecloths, 'masnad' (floor coverings) and yardage being the main articles of production. Hand-printing is also practised in Jammu city and the surrounding area.

The beautiful Vale of Kashmir is justly famed for its textiles, above all for the Kashmiri shawl. The foundations of the Kashmir shawl industry were traditionally believed to have been established by Zain-Ul-Abidin (1420–70), ruler of Kashmir, who was reputed to have brought weavers from Turkestan to the Valley. In the 'Ain-i-Akbari', the annals of the reign of the Mughal emperor Akbar (ruled 1556–1605), revealed that his wardrobes were full of shawls; many others served as highly prized gifts. Akbar introduced the fashion of wearing Kashmir shawls in pairs, stitched back to back, so that the undersides were never visible.

The origins and development of the Kashmir shawl owe much both to Kashmir's location, cut off as it is by the Pir Panjal range and to its position at the crossroads of some of Asia's great trade routes. Kashmir's relative geographical isolation ensured that a concentration of skilled workers could be built up and maintained. Its position on the trade routes from Tibet and from Turkestan gave it virtually exclusive use of the raw materials needed for shawls; and roads west to Afghanistan and Persia and south to India gave it access to markets for its textile products.

The classical Kashmir shawl was woven out of pashmina wool, whose main source was the fleece of a Central Asian species of mountain goat, the *Capra hircus*. This fleece grows, during the harsh, extremely cold winter, underneath the goat's outer hair and is shed at the beginning of summer. Pashmina wool was always imported from Tibet or Chinese Turkestan and was never produced in the Vale of Kashmir itself. There were two grades of pashmina. The finest grade was known as 'asli tus' and came from wild goats. The second grade came from the fleece of domesticated goats and it was this grade that always provided the main bulk of the yarn used by Kashmir looms.

Kashmir shawls were known as 'kani' shawls, and also as 'jamawars'. Woven in the twill-tapestry technique, the weft threads of these shawls alone form the pattern. They do not run across the full width of the cloth but are, by means of wooden spools known as 'tojli', woven back and forth across each section of the warp threads using the particular colour that that part of the pattern requires. Weaving a shawl in this way was a long, slow process. At the beginning of the nineteenth century, as shawl designs became more complex, work on a single shawl was split between two or more looms, thus cutting the length of time taken to weave the whole shawl; and as the nineteenth century progressed and designs became yet more complex, production was split between even more looms. The woven pieces were then sewn together by a 'rafugar'

(needleworker), with stitchery so fine as to make the joins virtually invisible.

The manufacture of shawls by such a lengthy and labour-intensive process meant that the finished article was very costly indeed. An Armenian named Khwaja Yusuf, who had come to Kashmir in 1803 as a buying agent for a Constantinople firm, introduced the concept of the 'amli', or needlework shawl, which would imitate the loom-woven shawl but would be much less expensive to produce and would escape the government duties levied on loom-

Corner of a 'phulkari' (shawl)

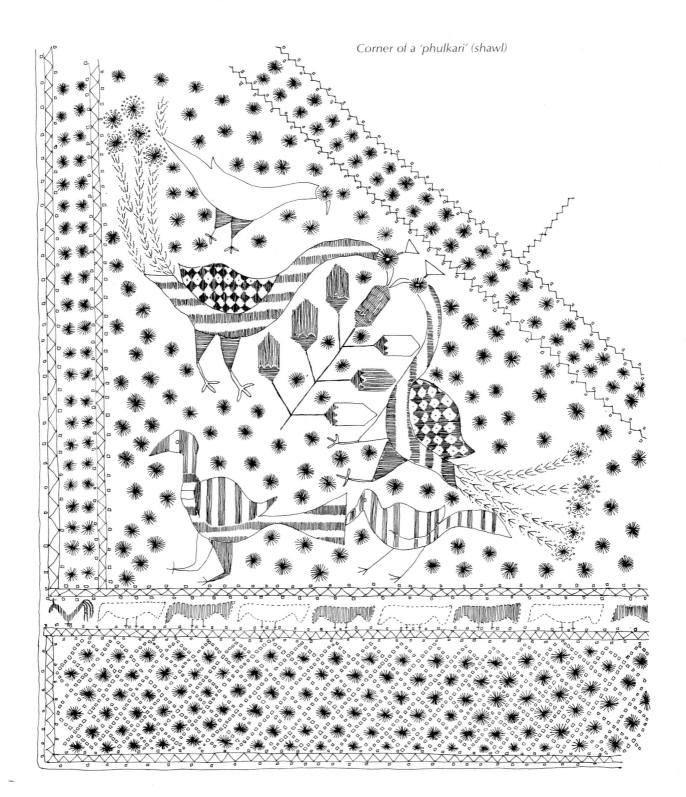

woven shawls. Between 1803 and 1823 the number of skilled embroiderers, who were also called 'rafugars', rose from a very few to nearly five thousand.

The shawl ground cloth was prepared by being rubbed with a piece of polished agate or cornelian on the flat surface of a plank until it was perfectly smooth. The pattern to be embroidered was then pounced on to the cloth with coloured powder or charcoal, and then embroidered in satin or stem stitch, each stitch made to lie as flat as possible by picking up warp threads individually. What was produced was a very fair imitation of the 'kani' or 'jamawar' loom-woven shawls. Maps of Srinagar were a favourite design and shawls embroidered with human figures were also very popular.

Production was in the hands of 'ustads' who owned the looms, and it has been recorded that the 'mokhuns', who were shawl brokers, acting between the loom owners and the foreign buyers, made the largest profits. The weavers, on the other hand, were underpaid, impoverished and oppressed by taxation and debt – to such an extent that many of them fled to the towns of the Punjab and what is now Himachal Pradesh to set up in business there.

The deterioration of the traditional Kashmir shawl production is well documented, and the saga of declining standards and of mass production resulting from the need to meet a foreign and seemingly limitless market demand is a salutary tale for folk craftwork world-wide. Exports created a fashion market in Europe and very soon stimulated competition from there. The first mention of an Indian woollen shawl being worn in Europe is in one of Lawrence Sterne's *Letters to Eliza* (1767). In the 1780s and 1790s, attempts were made first in Norwich, and then in Edinburgh, to imitate Kashmir shawls, and by 1808, weavers in Paisley were producing their own shawls to a Kashmir pattern. In response to this British initiative, production of Kashmir shawls was begun in Nîmes, Lyons and Alsace, in France.

By the beginning of the nineteenth century, Western Europe, and Napoleonic France in particular, was caught in the grip of an oriental romanticism. The wearing of genuine Kashmir shawls and their European replicas was highly fashionable; the colourful patterned borders of these shawls set off the plain textures of the classically inspired garments then in vogue. The Jacquard loom, first used in 1818 by French weavers, greatly simplified the weaving of complicated designs. Consequently, from 1818 on, the designs of French 'Kashmir' shawls became increasingly elaborate and covered a larger area of the fabric's surface. This in turn influenced the design of shawls in Kashmir.

Throughout the mid-nineteenth century, it was European, particularly French, taste that came to dominate shawl design in Kashmir. By 1850, French agents in Kashmir were setting out the designs and colours for the local weavers to follow, and between 1850 and 1860, shawl exports to Europe more than doubled; but this expansion was a prelude to the sudden collapse of the industry. Three important factors led to this collapse: firstly, Kashmir shawls could no longer compete in quality with the best Paisley and Lyons shawls. As patterns were dictated from Europe, there was a two-year gap between the design being sent out to Kashmir, and the return of the finished product, so that the latest shawls were already outmoded by the time they arrived. Kashmir shawls were also more expensive than those of Lyons and Paisley. Secondly, the Franco-Prussian War of 1870 meant the complete collapse of the French market for Kashmirs. Thirdly, Paisley and other imitation shawls were now cheap and plentiful, and much more likely to be worn by a working girl than by a member of the leisured classes. Thus, expensive Kashmir shawls were both priced out of the market and had lost the cachet and exclusivity of high fashion. The collapse of the industry in Kashmir was followed by a famine and the weavers were condemned to destitution and starvation. Only the needleworkers were able to salvage something by turning to the embroidery of coverlets, tablecloths and other domestic items for the home and tourist market.

Kashmir still produces many beautiful textiles, though most now have a uniformity of style that inevitably comes with catering to the mass market. There is today, however, output which has vivacity and individuality and matches masterful technique with the beauty of classical design. Kashmir shawls are still made all over the valley. The weaving of kani loom-woven pashmina shawls has been revived at the ancient weaving centre of Basohli in Jammu Province, but nearly all the Kashmir shawls made today are patterned by embroidery rather than by weaving. Only a fraction of these shawls are woven out of pashmina wool. The majority are made out of a yarn called 'raffal', introduced at the beginning of the twentieth century, which is spun out of merino wool. There are about one thousand handlooms weaving raffal shawls in Srinagar, as also are many powerlooms. In order to cut down on import costs, the rearing of pashmina-bearing goats is being encouraged in the high, arid Changthang region of Ladakh. With government help encouraging a more scientific breeding policy, yields are improving, and the nomadic

owners of the goats are also receiving a much better price for the pashmina, which should further improve production.

Whilst shawls are embroidered with a needle, much of the embroidery done in the Kashmir valley is ari work. As with the weaving, embroidery is a male profession. The ari work is used to decorate clothing, wall hangings, rugs, cushion covers and whole rolls of furnishing fabric, with varying complexity of design.

Himachal Pradesh

Himachal Pradesh is a mountain state that straddles the foothills and the high mountains of the Himalayas. The hill stations of this state are particularly well known, for Simla was the 'summer capital' of British India and the Kulu Valley is an idyllic escape from the summer heat of the plains. The Kulu Valley in particular is also associated with shawl weaving, but the state is best known for its embroidery arts that centre around the little town of Chamba.

From the early eighteenth century to the beginning of the twentieth, Chamba and its neighbouring hill states, such as Kangra and Basohli, formed the nucleus of 'rumal' production, embroidery work on thin unbleached muslin (mal-mal) of great charm and simplicity. 'Rumal' means 'cover' or 'kerchief', and these square-shaped textiles were used mainly as a covering for gifts. When an offering was made to temple gods, or gifts exchanged between the families of a bride and groom, an embroidered rumal was always used as wrapping. Chamba rumals were also used in temples and homes as a backdrop to, or canopy for, a deity. The region's rumals all shared the same basic composition, comprising a floral border which enclosed a finely drawn religious scene set against a clear, unembellished and unembroidered background. The designs were

initially drawn out in charcoal and featured scenes from Krishna's life and other mythological episodes, which were surrounded by clusters of willow and cypress trees and running animals such as tigers, horses and deer.

Chamba and its neighbouring hill states gave refuge to miniaturists of the imperial courts who fled to the hills at the break-up of the Mughal Empire during the eighteenth century. These painters were to found the school of 'Pahari' ('those of the hills') miniature painting. It was the Pahari school of painting that inspired the making of these textiles, but the miniatures themselves were not the direct source. Margaret Hall and John Irwin, in *Indian Embroideries*, propose that inspiration came from the murals painted by Pahari miniature painters on the walls of the Rang Mahal, the residence of the ladies at Chamba court. Ornate rumals were embroidered by ladies at the court with the designs most probably drafted by professional artists. In the village, meanwhile, women were embroidering the same articles in a much more primitive folk style.

Chamba rumals were embroidered in silks of soft colours, using small double-darning stitch, so that an identical design appeared evenly on both sides of the cloth, and double running stitch was used for outlines and details.

Uttar Pradesh

Uttar Pradesh is a state of overwhelming contrasts in a land where extremes are a normality. Densely populated – there are over ninety-eight million people, most of whom are poor farmers – the state is enriched and often flooded by the Ganges river. The Ganges dominates the state, emerging from the foothills of the Himalayas at Hardwar to

flow on to the vast expanse of plains, passing by the holiest city of all, Varanasi (formerly Benares). Fine woven brocades of precious metals from Varanasi and delicate whitework (embroidery using white thread upon fine white cotton fabric) from the capital, Lucknow, are the most famous textiles of Uttar Pradesh.

Chikan Work

Lucknow is a cultured city of beautiful buildings that lies at the centre of Uttar Pradesh. Now the capital of the modern state, in 1775 it had become the capital of the state of Oudh, when it at once began to attract craftsmen, artists and musicians who were patronized by the court. One of the crafts that developed was that of chikan-kari, or chikan-work embroidery, a kind of whitework. The pattern, of predominantly floral designs, is stitched using untwisted white cotton or silk (and now rayon) on the surface of the fabric. In chikan work, there is a fixed repertoire of stitches and it is usual for several types to appear on the same piece of embroidery.

'Moti' (beadwork) 'chakla' (square hanging)

Chikan work is thought to have originated in Bengal and to have been practised in Dacca and Calcutta. The jamdani weaving of Dacca must have been influential, as also eighteenth-century European whitework. The visual effect of a jamdani weave is of a series of flowers or geometric designs, set against a semi-translucent mesh background. Bengali chikan work produced the same kind of effect through embroidery – a method both simpler and cheaper than the more skilled weaving process. (Here indeed, a parallel can be drawn with the introduction of embroidered shawls in Kashmir at the beginning of the nineteenth century.) It is worth noting in this respect that while jamdani weaving was previously confined to Dacca, from 1850 onwards very fine white-on-white jamdani was produced in Tanda, near Faizabad, to the east of Lucknow; to which period Hall and Irwin, in *Indian*

Embroideries, ascribe the beginnings of the Lucknow chikan-kari industry. Bengali chikan work consisted mainly of piece goods for trade ('tepchi' – a long running stitch worked from the top side to produce the myriad trailing flower stems of Lucknow chikan-kari – was used in Bengal to imitate jamdani patterning).

Normally, fine white stranded cotton is used for chikan embroidery. Some stitches are worked from the front of the fabric, others from the back. Sheila Paine, in *Chikan Embroidery*, observes that there are six basic stitches, which are used in combination with a series of stitches for embossing flowers and leaves. Pulledwork (known in chikan work by the Hindi word 'jali', which means 'a window with a pierced lattice, which can be looked out of but not into') and 'khatao' (an appliqué-and-cut technique, where one piece of fabric is hemmed on to another piece and then cut away) complete the repertoire.

Now all the fabric used is mill-made, and cotton/polyester mixtures and thin silk are used in addition to cotton. Certainly the nature of the chikan-work industry has changed out of all recognition since the beginning of the twentieth century. The quality of chikan work suffered a catastrophic decline due to the loss of patronage from the courts and the 'zamindar' (landlords), and the industry became orientated towards the mass market – the last two great master embroiderers died in Lucknow in the early 1980s. Whilst there are still embroiderers who work to commission, the vast majority of the work remains cheap and rough, and is used to decorate the 'salwar-kameez' (suit) and other garments that are exported abroad and sold cheaply all over the bazaars of India.

The Brocades of Varanasi

The town known by its ancient religious name as Kasi, by its present Sanskritized name of Varanasi, and more colloquially as Benares, lies athwart the Ganges and is one of the oldest continually inhabited places in the world. It is one of the four most important places of Hindu pilgrimage, and an auspicious place to die and to begin again the cycle of rebirth. The city is a warren of alleys and gulleys leading down to the bathing and burning ghats of the river through a network of tiny shops, temples and 'dharmsalas' (places of rest) for pilgrims.

Alaipura is traditionally the district of Varanasi where the famous Benares brocades are woven, though they are now also woven in other parts of the city. Brocades are textiles woven with warp and weft threads of different colours and often of different materials. The Benares brocades are woven in silk, with profuse use of metal threads on the 'pallavs' (endpieces) and the field of the sari. The weavers are Muslim, but, significantly, they are not known by the common word for weaver, 'jullaha', but as 'karigar', which means 'artist'. The brocades are woven in workshops known as 'karkhanahs' which are a series of interconnecting rooms, usually on the first floor. Almost every square inch of ground space in the room is taken up with looms, and above each loom hangs a crowded arrangement of strings leading down to the loom heddles. The weavers work in artificial light (nowadays, by an electric light), in a calm and quiet atmosphere which is conducive to the concentration needed for the weaving of such complicated designs.

The zari thread, known as 'kalabattun', consists of finely drawn gold, silver or base metal thread, wound round a silk thread. Silk traditionally came from Bengal, Central Asia and Italy, but now comes from either Malda, in Bengal, or from Kashmir or Japan. Varanasi paradoxically lies within a cotton-growing area, and although there is documentary evidence of cotton textiles dating back to the first millennium BC, there is no mention of silk brocades until Tavernier's description of his visit to Varanasi in AD 1665, from which can be surmised that the textiles he saw in the caravanserais and temples were Varanasi zari-work brocades. The East India Company arrived in Varanasi in 1764 and took over the administration soon afterwards. Varanasi then became a haven for many rich merchants and noble families escaping from the troubles of post-Mughal north India. These were the clients who patronized the Benares zari and brocade maufacturers, and demanded textiles of the type of fineness which gave the Benares brocades their name. According to local legend, Varanasi was one of the centres to which brocade weaving was brought after a great fire in Gujarat in 1300.

The most famous brocaded textile of Varanasi is called 'kinkhab' (a Persian term), woven with a coarse but durable silk known as 'mukta' which is heavy enough to take brocading with gold or silver thread. Kinkhab was also woven at other centres, notably Ahmedabad and Surat in Gujarat and at Paithan, Aurangabad and Hyderabad in the Deccan. Kinkhab was a heavy fabric, often used for furnishing but rarely for clothing, and was not only a popular trading article on the local market, but was also exported to Europe. A silk-and-zari-work brocade of lighter material and less heavy ornamentation is known as 'pot-than' or 'bafta'. The name for brocades without any metal thread work is 'amaru'.

Benares brocades are woven on pitlooms. Traditionally, the design of the brocade was first worked out on paper and then an expert, known as a 'naksha bandha', rendered the design into cotton threads on a 'naksha' (the indigenous thread device that performs the same function as the Jacquard). The naksha bandhas of Varanasi were so skilled that they tied the designs for the weavers of other brocading centres, such as Surat in Gujarat and Chanderi in Madhya Pradesh. Today in Varanasi, the Jacquard device has overwhelmingly replaced the use of the naksha.

The delicate designs of the past were replaced at the end of the nineteenth century by patterns taken from Victorian sample books of English wallpaper. These very heavy designs have now been largely superseded by patterns inspired by the folk art of Assam, Bengal and Gujarat, and adaptations of Mughal, Rajasthani and Pahari paintings. Varanasi sari brocades, deep-coloured and laden with gold thread, are the popular wedding attire for wealthy Indian brides.

The densely populated north of India has a proud textile tradition, but there is not nearly so strong a local demand from the rural population for hand-produced textiles as there is in west India. Contemporary phulkaris and Chamba rumals are very rare indeed. Rural life has changed irrevocably and no longer is there time or need for the working of these beautiful textiles. The commercial chikan-work embroidery long ago lost the rich patrons who would commission the work, leaving it an industry dedicated to the decoration of cheap garments for the foreign and domestic markets.

The remaining strengths of the northern textile tradition are the commercial embroidery and weaving of Kashmir and the commercial brocade weaving of Varanasi. Both have strong mass markets, which provide a base within which textiles, of technical excellence and beautiful design, rival the products of the past.

Silk and metal thread brocade sari from Varanasi

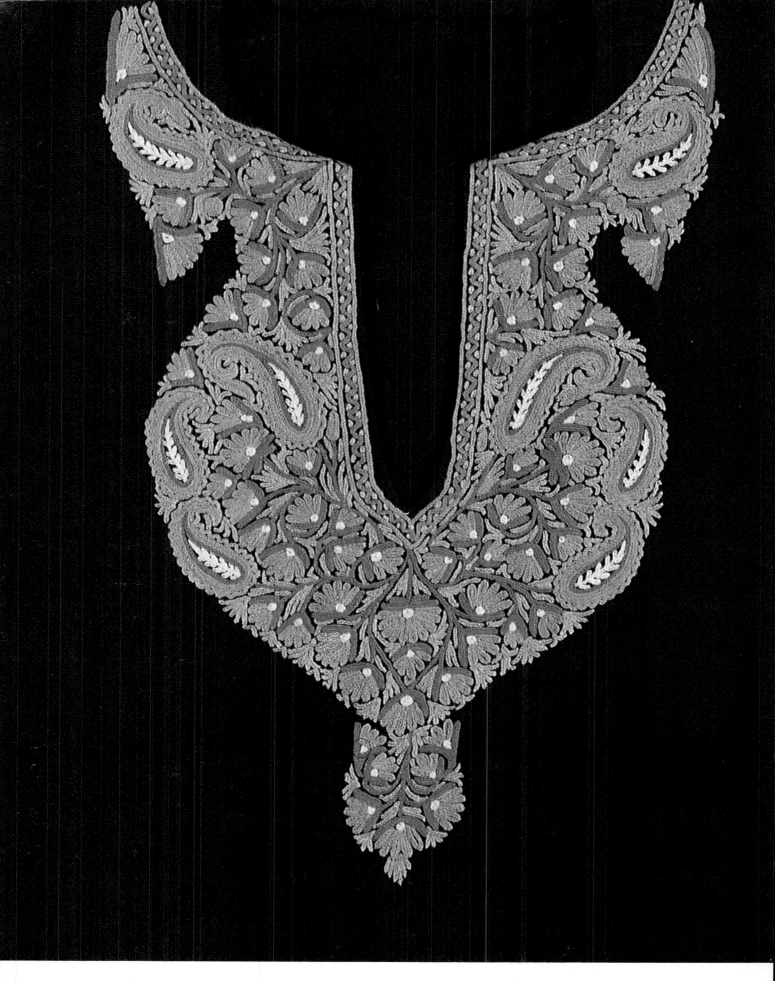

Kashmiri ari-work embroidery on a 'phiren' (smock) yoke

Stole brocaded with gold and silken thread from Varanasi

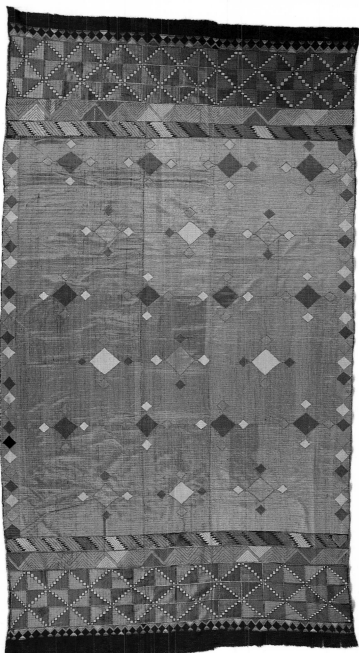

'Bagh' (wedding shawl), embroidered with silk on cotton, east Punjab

(Opposite) Detail of a cotton tablecloth with silk embroidery, from Kashmir

Bagh displaying the wave pattern known as 'leheria', from west Punjab

Sheep-washing at Dal Lake, Srinagar, Kashmir

'Gaghra' (skirt) displaying the phulkari work of the Bishnui caste of Bhantinda/ Hissar District, Punjab/Haryana border (Opposite) 'Phulkari' (woman's shawl) with silk embroidery on 'khaddar' cotton cloth, east Punjab

(Below) Appliqué hanging made for the contemporary tourist market (in the Delhi area) in apparent imitation of the 'kanduri' cloths that have long been offered to the shrine of Salar Masud, the warrior nephew of Mahmud of Ghazni at Bahraich, Uttar

Pradesh. This hanging features the 'dargah' shrine, with figures of warriors above but surrounded by figures derived from Hindu iconography reflecting the syncretic nature of the Salar Masud cult.

Cotton sari with extra weft patterning, from Kanchipuram, Tamil Nadu

6　The East and The South

The eastern region of the Subcontinent, the states of Bihar, West Bengal, Orissa, Assam, the adjoining hill states and the country of Bangladesh (previously East Bengal) are less prosperous than western India, but rich in a culture that has a very ancient history. Bihar and West Bengal are densely populated areas of flat plains traversed by the river Ganges, which spread north to the foothills of the Himalayas. Assam and Meghalaya are hill states abutting the Brahma Putra valley whose inhabitants exhibit strong connections with the tribally dominated societies of Arunachal Pradesh, Nagaland, Manipur, Tripura and Mizoram. Orissa is a largely unspoilt state of farming villages with a relatively small population, best known for the great religious centre of Puri and the ancient temples of Bhubaneswar and Konarak. In the past it was isolated from the rest of India by the thick forests of its hills.

Bengal and Bihar

Old, undivided Bengal had an ancient textile tradition, rooted above all in the skilled weaving of delicate muslins and the folk embroidery of quilts. The fine mal-mals and jamdanis of Dacca, and the 'Baluchar' brocade saris of Murshidabad with their pictorial borders, were prized products, as were the embroidered quilts, intricately worked with scenes of Portuguese inspiration (featuring, for example, armoured men on horseback) in the wild silk native to Bengal and Assam, and exported to Europe in the seventeenth century. These were textiles that sought to adapt themselves to the demands of a wide market, both in India and abroad.

In the sphere of folk textiles the needleworked quilts of Bengal and Bihar form a group of some of the most interesting cloths of the Subcontinent. They are known as 'kanthas' in Bengal and as 'sujanis' in Bihar. In the past they were made for family use or as gifts, out of cast-off saris or dhotis. Saris and dhotis in this area are predominantly white, sometimes with a border in black or red, or blue and red, sometimes with the addition of yellow or green. Three or four sections of sari or dhoti were laid on top of each other and then quilted. The simple running stitch used in quilting produces an embroidery-like design whose details were filled in with satin and stem stitch. Threads were taken from the coloured borders of the saris or dhotis for this purpose.

The conventional pattern of Bengal kanthas had a lotus medallion in the centre (symbolizing the universe) and four 'buttis', or trees, at the corners. The rest of the field was then embroidered with all manner of motifs: birds, fish, animals and people, with domestic scenes mixed in with religious and allegorical figures. Very rarely were two kanthas ever alike. The distinguished textile scholar Stella Kramrisch believes the inspiration for these textiles lies in the 'alpona' designs, which are drawn out on the floor and doorstep in Bengal at festival times. Indeed, it is easy to see the relationship of the simple sujanis of north Bihar to the wall paintings of the local district of Madubhani.

Kanthas were used as winter quilts, covers and wraps for books and valuables, as mats for ceremonial purposes. Kantha-making for home consumption in Bengal died out by about the end of the first quarter of the twentieth century due to the usual pressures of industrialization (West Bengal was then the most industrialized state in India) and changes in rural life. The main centres for kantha-making were in East Bengal, now Bangladesh, where it has now been revived. Here embroidered, quilted hangings are made with new cloth to some of the old designs, the best of them expressing some of the lively views of nature of the old classics. These new kanthas are aimed at the export and tourist market.

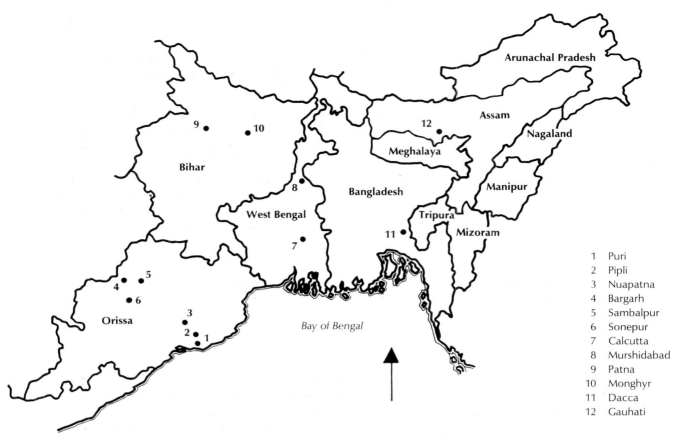

Northern Bihar is a land of rich and fertile soil, but due to the lack of industrialization, a harsh landlord system and the damaging effects of recurring floods, there is much poverty. It has always been an isolated area, even in Mughal times, and has retained folk crafts of a very distinctive style, unaffected by outside influences. Its textile crafts include not only the embroidered and quilted sujani work but also the chain-stitch embroidery of Monghyr District. Indeed, all over Bihar, women embroider blouses, saris or shawls, sashes, babies' caps and pillow-covers, for personal use and for their families. Appliqué, both for commercial and for domestic purposes, is produced round Patna and in northern Bihar. There are two different types of appliqué that are still commonly practised. One is called 'khatwa', whereby patterns are cut into a complete piece of cloth, which is then appliquéd to a background cloth. With the other method, a pattern is formed with single motifs of cloth or edging strips which are then individually appliquéd.

Assam and the Hill States of the North-East

The north-east of India consists of the states of Assam, through which flows the vast, turbulent Brahmaputra river, Meghalaya with its hill stations and tea gardens, and the tribally dominated hill states of Arunachal Pradesh, Nagaland, Manipur, Tripura and Mizoram which are the border states with China, Burma and Bangladesh. The region has many affinities with its neighbours to the east, and its indigenous peoples are markedly different from those of the north Indian plains and Bangladesh.

Short staple cotton and the wild silks known as 'muga' and 'eri' are produced in Assam, and the whole of the north-east is noted for its weaving, be it for the beautifully balanced, intricate patterns of the commercial cloth of Assam and Manipur, or for the diverse, often boldly patterned fabrics of the domestic looms in each of the north-east states. Handloom-weaving is Assam's largest and oldest industry.

Unlike the rest of India, women form the bulk of the weavers throughout the north-east. Mahatma Gandhi once commented: 'Assamese women are born weavers, they can weave fairy-tales in their cloth.' Indeed, in Assamese tradition, a girl was not considered marriageable until she had proved herself a proficient weaver. To this end, she would weave a towel called a 'bihuan' and present it to her beloved. These towels are white, patterned at both ends, usually in red, with stylized forms of birds, animals, humans, flowers, foliage and geometric motifs.

For domestic production, a throw shuttle loom is used in the non-tribal lowlands and a backstrap loom by the hill tribes. Commercial weaving, which is centred at Sualkuchi, Raha, Palasbiri and at other centres in Assam and Manipur, is done on flyshuttle looms, with the aid of a Jacquard device. In the north-east there is no specific weaving caste except among the Bengali immigrants, who use the pitloom. The commercial operations have their yarn dyed at local establishments, whereas the hill tribes have indigenous methods of colouring their yarn and textiles, using locally available natural dye sources such as bark, seeds, flowers and the leaves of trees. Cotton, 'pat' (mulberry) silk and 'muga' and 'eri' (non-mulberry) silk are the basic raw materials used. Assam produces two-thirds of India's non-mulberry silk, and the area has an ancient history of sericulture, most probably brought into the Assam region by the migrating Bodo and related tribes. All Assamese women wear some articles of silk at their weddings. Weaving amongst the tribal societies is a home craft, using a simple backstrap loom of the kind found in Indonesia. The textiles produced are simple, striped fabrics sometimes decorated with needle weaving and with shells, seeds, beads and pieces of metal. Patterns can be geometric or figurative.

Orissa

Orissa is a beautiful state, well irrigated by rivers, its landscape rising up from the temple towns of the coast through the Eastern Ghats with their thick forests, to the Deccan plateau. The women of Orissa dress in saris of blue, red and magenta and other deep colours, with ikat (known as 'bandha' in Orissa) patterning. The men wear ikat lungis and have smaller ikat cloths draped over their shoulders. All this cloth is made within the state, either at Nuapatna, near Cuttack on the coastal plain, or in the weaving centres inland around Sambalpur and Sonepur.

In the villages around Sambalpur, Bargarh and Sonepur the weavers are predominantly members of the Meher caste. They claim that their forefathers originally came from Rajasthan or Delhi by way of Madhya Pradesh. The Mehers now weave complicated designs in cotton, mainly using weft ikat, with sometimes warp ikat for the borders and, less often, double ikat for parts of the central field and the pallav. Patterns seem to have greatly increased in complexity from relatively simple beginnings as this century has progressed. The textile that is traditionally the pride of this area is the saktapar sari, with its double ikat chequerboard pattern and brocaded border of 'rudraksha' bead compositions. The development of these fabrics has been much encouraged by local patronage. The weavers have, until recent times, had a local market which was insulated, because of difficulties of transport, from the temptations of mill-made cloth.

This century there has been much cross-fertilization between the Sambalpur–Sonepur region and Nuapatna. The weavers of Sambalpur–Sonepur have the technical expertise to tie and dye and weave silk, but rarely do so. At Nuapatna, cotton has been tied and dyed and woven only from the middle of this century, but is still much cruder than the products of Sambalpur–Sonepur. Cloth is woven on pitlooms in Orissa. In both areas, the layout of the textile design takes the form of horizontal stripes, and motifs are mainly floral or of fish and animals, rarely geometrical.

Pipli is a small village on the main road between Bhubaneswar and Puri, and from Pipli comes much brightly coloured appliqué work. Like Nuapatna, Pipli has strong connections with the Jagannath temple at Puri. Temple records state that in 1054 Maharajah Birakshore of Puri appointed tailors of the Darji caste as 'sebaks', to provide a regular supply of appliquéd articles for the daily sebas (rites performed in the temple). Pilgrims coming to Puri would stop at Pipli to buy banners as offerings to the temple gods, and on their way home they would purchase souvenir bags or small canopies for their domestic deities and for festivals in their own town. As well as making articles for the Jagannath temples and for the pilgrims, the Darjis of Pipli supplied the 'maths', or monastic houses, with appliquéd articles for their religious processions. Since Independence, however, with the decline of the maths and the loss of patronage from the Rajah of Puri, the Darjis of Pipli have taken to making articles for the tourist trade, such as cushion covers and bedspreads.

Travelling southwards from the mountains and valleys of the Himalayan foothills, the desert landscapes and fortified towns of western India, or from the crowded Gangetic floodplains, one enters into another world, a world of the southern peoples. There is a great variety of cultures reflected in this region of diverse landscapes, which ranges from tropical plantations to barren boulder-strewn plateaux. In Andhra Pradesh the Mughal Empire reached the limit of its expansion into the once powerful Hindu kingdoms; Tamil Nadu is a colourful state packed with examples of Dravidian art and architecture; and Kerala shelters in the shadow of the Western Ghats as a fertile strip of coastal land whose people have mingled with alien seaborne traders, exiles and adventurers for thousands of years. The legacy of Jewish, early Christian,

Arabic, Chinese, Portuguese, Dutch and English cultures abound in the robust and extroverted communities of the coastal south. To the north, Karnataka is a glorious mix of Islamic and Hindu influences, home to the ruins of Hampi, centre of the largest Hindu kingdom of all time. Reaching out into the high Deccan plateau, Maharashtra is a large and populous state proud of its cosmopolitan capital, Bombay, and of its historical connections with the warlike Marathas of the past. In textile traditions, the south is well remembered for its printed and painted export cloths: the 'pintadoes' and the chintzes that furnished the drawing rooms of seventeenth-century Europe with the exotic; for its telia rumal headcloths exported to the Muslim world; and for its silk weaving of the deep-coloured saris which form the garb of southern women.

Ikats of Andhra Pradesh

Chirala is a village near the coast of Andhra Pradesh, between the rail junction of Vijayawada and the city of Madras. Here were produced the square double-ikated cloths known as telia, or Asia, rumals. These were produced for the Muslim market (to be used mainly as headcloths by Muslim men), sold in what is now Pakistan and Bangladesh and exported to the countries of the Middle East, East Africa and to Burma. In Chirala, telia rumals were dyed with traditional alizarin dyes, which left an oily smell from which their name derives. Designs were either geometrical or figurative, sometimes of clocks and aeroplanes. Today, the few surviving weavers supply local customers such as fishermen, who use the telia rumals as lungis, or as turbans. After the partition of India in 1947, the market for telia rumals in Pakistan and Bangladesh was lost, and in the second half of the twentieth century, demand for them from the Middle East vanished completely.

Whereas ikat weaving (known as 'chitka' in Andhra Pradesh) is apparently in terminal decline

in Chirala, it is flourishing in Pochampalli and surrounding villages. Pochampalli is a large village, about fifty-five kilometres from Hyderabad, the historic capital of Andhra Pradesh. According to the head of the society of co-operative weavers at Pochampalli, weaving there was originally dedicated to the production of plain dhotis and saris, with simple patterned borders. The weaving of telia rumals was then introduced, most probably from Chirala, and the techniques of ikating, once learned, were then applied to the weaving of saris, dupattas and yardage. Pochampalli uses only modern synthetic dyes, unlike Chirala, which still uses alizarin dyes. Pochampalli and its surrounding villages have very active co-operatives and private master weavers. The main bulk of private sector production is of saris, and the co-ops produce both saris and yardage. Probably because of the comparative youth of the ikat industry, the Pochampalli weaving centres are some of the most outward-looking of all traditional textile producers in India. Double- and single-ikat saris of the patola patterns of Gujarat are woven and much of the yardage is devoted to ikat patterns taken from Orissa, Japan and even Central Asia. There is a good local and all-India market for saris, though the women of Andhra Pradesh do not provide such an overwhelmingly strong local market as in Orissa. Much of the yardage is aimed at export trade. Traditional ikat fabrics of Andhra Pradesh use at the most three colours, forming simple geometric designs and, as in Orissa, are woven on pitlooms.

Kalamkari Work of South-Eastern India

The Coromandel coast of India, stretching from Masulipatnam to the north down to Nagapatnam in the south, was historically the source of some of the most beautifully coloured and delicately worked cotton fabrics produced and exported by India. Unlike the Gujarat area, the other great historic source of Indian export textiles, where printing with blocks was the main means of patterning, on the south-east coast dyes, mordants and resists were traditionally applied with a brush or pen. Figurative and floral designs of great fineness were possible using this method of drawing and painting.

Before the European merchants' incursion into the Indian commercial world, the main export market for south-east Indian textiles was in South-East Asia, to what is now Malaysia, Indonesia and the Philippines. The Europeans, whose main purpose was to obtain spices in South-East Asia, soon realized that the spice islanders were more interested in Indian cloth than in precious metals as a medium of exchange for their spices. Consequently, the European merchants began to use their limited stocks of gold and silver to buy in bulk the beautiful and inexpensive textiles of the south-east Indian coast. The ships would arrive from Europe, anchor in such ports as Masulipatnam for up to a year, fill up with cloth and then set out on the second leg of their three-part trip to pick up spices. If they could manage to get back to Europe safely, they would indeed make a more than handsome profit.

1	Bombay
2	Nagpur
3	Jalgaon
4	Aurangabad
5	Paithan
6	Hyderabad
7	Pochampalli
8	Masulipatnam
9	Chirala
10	Kalahasti
11	Madras
12	Thanjavur
13	Kumbakonam
14	Madurai
15	Kanchipuram
16	Ootacamund
17	Quilon
18	Trivandrum
19	Trichur
20	Cochin
21	Bangalore

Masulipatnam was then under the rule of the Shia Muslim Qutbshahi dynasty of Golconda (near modern Hyderabad) which had links with the Safavid of Persia. It was probably around this time that cloth from Masulipatnam started to be exported to Iran. The painted cloth of south-east India had been known as 'pintado' by the Portuguese and 'chintz' by the English. It was, however, the Persian link that gave the painted cloths the name of 'kalamkari', by which they have been known in India from medieval times to the present day. 'Kalam' is a Persian word, meaning 'pen', and 'kari' means 'work'.

There was a decline in the European demand for spices during the seventeenth and eighteenth centuries due to dietary changes in Europe lessening dependence on salted meat as a winter staple; and so the English, French and Dutch East India companies began flooding the European market with cottons of bright and fast colours. The Europeans, hitherto restricted to a narrow range of fugitive colours, had such an appetite for this new material that from the mid-seventeenth century through most of the eighteenth, European demand kept the kalamkari workers of the coast at full stretch.

The European cotton industry established in the eighteenth century was to sound the death knell of the kalamkari chintz industry. Workers were thrown into penury, and master craftsmen died without heirs to their trade secrets. The rise of the batik industry in nineteenth-century Indonesia lost south-east India that market for cloth. In the nineteenth century what remained was the export market to Persia and indigenous demand for narrative cloths on scrolls, from temples and local zamindars. Much reduced in scale as it is, the kalamkari industry that exists today has been shaped by these two markets.

Masulipatnam, with its historic Persian links, concentrated on this market. Motifs used were, amongst others, the Persian-derived 'butti' or Paisley cone, and the 'mihrab' which, as they were often repeated, lent themselves to block work. Around the mid-nineteenth century, printing blocks were introduced, and from then on very little freehand kalam drawing was done. Large figurative kalamkari wall-hangings for both the foreign and domestic markets were formerly made at Pulicat, near Madras, and Palakollu, near Masulipatnam.

The small temple town of Sri Kalahasti in the extreme south-east corner of the modern state of Andhra Pradesh only became an important centre for kalamkari in the nineteenth century. Local legend has it that a kalamkari worker from Nellore, who was partial to drink, was plied with liquor for days until he had divulged all his secrets. Be that as it may, Kalahasti was well placed for kalamkari work, as it lay on the river Swarnamukhi, which was favourable for dyeing operations and could enjoy the great patronage of the famous temple town of Tirupati. The textile scholar Lotika Varadarajan, in her book *Kalamkari*, attributes the layouts of the Kalahasti kalamkari cloths to the narrative mural paintings of the temples of the Vijayanagar Empire, and more immediately to the murals of Nataraja Ranga Salam just outside the main temple at Kalahasti. The kalamkari workers of Kalahasti worked under the patronage of local temples, who demanded strongly figurative and narrative components, with all the different gods and goddesses and accompanying figures. Certainly there is a religious colour code for the decoration of kalamkari cloths – all gods are blue, female characters are golden yellow, bad characters and demons are red. This free style of pictorial expression called for the use of the kalam; its minimal use of repeats was never suited to block work.

Production at both Masulipatnam and Kalahasti fell into steep decline at the beginning of the twentieth century. In 1924, Persia prohibited the import of Indian kalamkari. The period from 1924 up to Independence and beyond saw the near-disappearance of the industry at Masulipatnam. At the same time, at Kalahasti, temple patronage declined and the local landlords lost wealth and powers of patronage. In 1952, kalamkari was revived at Masulipatnam at the instigation of some local textile-lovers and with the aid of the All India Handicrafts Board. The kalamkari, as used and made in Iran, was taken as a model. The use of indigo was eschewed as the painting-on of the wax resist was so time-consuming. A minimum of colour was used, with an emphasis on the filling-in of fine details with a kalam after the pattern had been block printed.

In Kalahasti, in 1958, the All India Handicrafts Board set up a training course and school for kalamkari workers, drawing on the skills of the few remaining workers. Production in Masulipatnam is now aimed mainly at the domestic market, and in Kalahasti at the foreign tourist market.

The Silk Industry of Kanchipuram

Kanchipuram, in Tamil Nadu, is a famous temple town forty-seven miles south-west of Madras. It was the capital city of the Pallava Empire, in the latter part of the first millennium AD, and then became part of the Chola and Vijayanagar Empires. Kanchipuram produces brocaded silks of superb texture, colour and lustre. As in many weaving centres, the workers say that the weaving of silk developed from that of weaving cotton through a series of intermediate stages. The raw mulberry silk used is brought in from the Bangalore area, which has ideal climatic conditions for the rearing of mulberry silk worms. Zari threads for brocading come from Surat, Gujarat. The dull raw silk yarn is washed in the waters of Kanchipuram. It is this water which gives Kanchipuram silk its lustrous sheen.

The main items of production are the silk saris with the solid brocaded borders ('korvai'); silk yardage is also produced. The silk is woven on a throw shuttle pitloom with a drawboy harness. Designs and patterns are woven with extra warp and weft, and are worked into the body of the fabric by means of an indigenous device known as the 'adai', which fulfils the same function as the Jacquard. Kanchipuram saris in the south Indian style have a pallav and/or borders that contrast in colour to the main field of the sari. Although methods of weaving are traditional, Kanchipuram textiles have attained their current status by always keeping pace with changes in popular preference and taste. It is in this capacity that the role of the Weaving Service Centre set up at Kanchipuram by the All India Handicrafts Board has been vital.

Tamil Nadu has a very strong cotton handloom industry organized into co-operatives. Cotton lungis and yardage, mainly in checks, are woven in villages all over Tamil Nadu. Arni is known for its handwoven textiles, Madras, Thanjavur and Madurai are centres for hand-printed textiles and Madurai also for tie-and-dye work. The towns of Salem, Erode and Kumbakonam are centres for both handwoven and hand-printed cloth. Appliqué hangings, banners and decorations for temple carts used to be made in and near Thanjavur. Felt materials, or velvet, were appliquéd to a cotton background and the appliquéd patterns were then edged with cotton cords. The background colour was usually red, with pieces of cream, green, yellow and black cloth being used for the appliquéd pieces. The central motifs were usually of Ganesh, Lakshmi or other deities surrounded by floral motifs. Appliquéd cloths are now prepared in the Thanjavur–Madurai area, to be sold mainly to the tourist market.

The Todas of the Nilgiri hills around Ootacamund are a small tribe, very different in both appearance and customs to the surrounding Tamil communities. Both men and women wear a shawl of white cotton, usually about nine yards long, called a 'putkulli'. The end of this shawl has two woven bands of either red and black, or red and indigo blue. Toda women embroider geometric designs between these two bands to give the shawl a striking pallav. The embroidery is worked by counting threads and follows the warp and weft threads of the material, giving the impression that the patterning is achieved through weaving rather than by embroidery.

Kerala, Karnataka, Goa and Maharashtra

Kerala has a tradition of lace-making and embroidery that has a strong European influence. Handloomed textiles are woven at Cannanore, Palghat, Kottayam and Trivandrum and cotton textiles (mainly batik and screen-printed lungis) are printed at Trichur, Quilon and Trivandrum.

Karnataka is famous for its silk work, and Bangalore and Kollegal are both centres of silk sari-weaving in the southern style. Strong, durable cotton handloomed textiles are produced at

Bijapur and Guledagud. Of special interest, however, is the 'kasuti' embroidery. Such embroidery is done by Kannada-speaking women in parts of Maharashtra and Karnataka, who make interesting use of very simple stitchery. Young girls embroider cholis and the pallavs of saris for their marriage trousseaus using different varieties of running stitch. Designs are built up in squares and triangles, to form delicate patterns of stylized flowers, animals, birds and even temple carts. The designs are worked in cotton or silk thread, in colours which harmonize with the background cloth. Kasuti work, like the kantha work of Bengal, was a domestic craft which had declined but has now been revived on a commercial basis.

Goa is noted for its European-influenced embroidery, the production of which has received a boost, due to the influx of tourists over recent years.

'Himroo' is a cotton warp and silk weft brocade produced at Aurangabad, Maharashtra. The silk weft only appears on the surface to form the usually floral pattern, leaving the rest of the weft hanging loose underneath. Himroo fabric is woven on a throw shuttle pitloom, and patterning is achieved by using a device known as a 'jala', which consists of a bunch of threads hanging down from the ceiling which are attached to the warp threads, so that they are lifted in the required order. The gauze-like saris of Paithan, near Aurangabad, are woven of heavy gold brocade where, in reverse of the usual brocading practice, the metal zari threads form the background, and the pattern details are in silk.

Banjara Embroidery

The Banjaras are a tribe of north Indian origin, who moved south into the Deccan plateau during the seventeenth century as carters in the baggage train of the Mughal emperor Aurangzeb. The Banjaras had to abandon their ancestral profession as carters, due to the British railway-building during the nineteenth century. They now live in small villages called 'tandas' throughout the Deccan plateau, and work mainly as casual labourers. Banjara women always wear their finest clothes and jewelry, even when doing hard manual labour on building sites or breaking up stones for public roads.

Banjara embroidery is noted for its lively decoration – cowrie shells, coins, cotton and woollen tassels weighted with lead and glass beads and mirrorwork are all used to adorn their textiles. The Banjara women of Andhra Pradesh wear gaghras, cholis and odhnis in bold appliqué and mirrorwork; more subtle is the work of the Banjara of Madhya Pradesh and adjoining areas in Maharashtra and Karnataka. The Banjara to be found in Malwa and Nimar districts of Madhya Pradesh and across into Maharashtra towards Jalgaon produce beautiful work made up of squares and rectangles of cross and stem stitch, contained within a grid laid out in closely worked herring-bone stitch. Designs are either geometric or angularly zoomorphic. The most common articles produced are the square, tasselled rumals (kerchiefs) edged with cowries, which are used for presentations at ceremonies and in ceremonial dances; purses ('batua') for money or areca nuts; and cholis, gaghras and odhnis are also embroidered.

Other Banjara make beautiful, quilted rumals, bags and purses, usually on brown or sometimes blue cloth. Patterning is sometimes confined to quilting stitches, but more usually cotton threads are laid on in contrasting geometric patterns, and then couched down. Further south, the Banjara work some of the most intricate embroidery, using woollen or cotton thread and a great repertoire of stitches, making bags, purses, waist bands and a rectangular piece of embroidery edged with cowrie shells, which hangs down from a head ring called an 'indhoni' on which the women balance pots of water.

Eastern and southern India both have very strong weaving traditions. In common with other parts of India, in many of the villages the weavers produce simple handloom fabrics for the needs of the rural population. Regardless of whether the weaver lives in Bihar or Tamil Nadu, he will be weaving cloth for the same purpose, for saris and shawls, dhotis and lungis. The colours and style of embellishment of these textiles are dictated by climatic and cultural factors, and in areas which heretofore had rich and courtly patrons, sophisticated textiles of complex technique and design have evolved over the centuries from the original, simple style.

Length of nineteenth-century 'mashru' yardage from the Deccan

Drawing out a design with a kalam pen, in Kalahasti, Andhra Pradesh

'Kalamkari' (pen-work) cloth depicting a scene from the Mahabharata epic, in which Krishna recites the Bhagavad Gita to Arjuna in his chariot before the battle of Kurukshetra. From Kalahasti, Andhra Pradesh.

(Opposite) Section of contemporary kalamkari cloth, from Masulipatnam, Andhra Pradesh

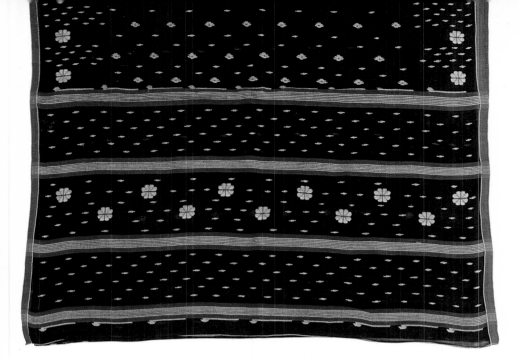

Sari known by the trade name 'Tangail', made with the 'jamdani' technique, from west Bengal

(Opposite) Weft-ikat sari with warp ikat and brocade borders, from Sambalpur District, Orissa

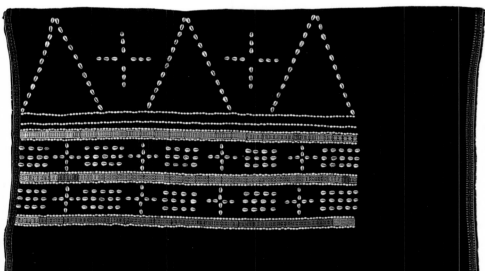

Shawl with metal and cowrie-shell decorations, probably of the Naga from Nagaland or Arunachal Pradesh

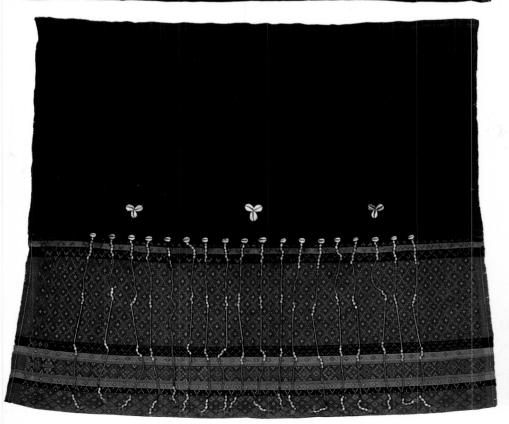

Apron with woven border, decorated with cowrie shells, beads and rolled-up sections of tin cans, from the Indian-Burmese border region

Winding yarn on to a bobbin for weft work, in Barpali, Orissa

Preparing the yarn for dyeing by resist binding, in Barpali, Orissa

(Opposite) Detail of single-ikat silk sari, probably from Pochampalli, Andhra Pradesh

Marking out the weft threads for tying, before dyeing, in Pochampalli, Andhra Pradesh

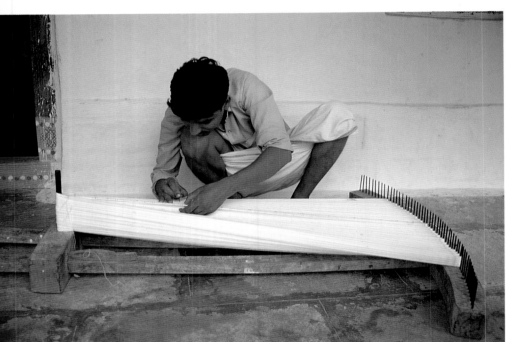

(Bottom left) Prepared yarn on a dyeing frame, in Pochampalli, Andhra Pradesh

(a)   Double-ikat cotton 'rumal' (cover, or kerchief), made at Puttapaka village, near Hyderabad, Andhra Pradesh; and (b) and (c) 'telia rumal' double-ikat cloths from Puttapaka village, near Hyderabad, Andhra Pradesh

a

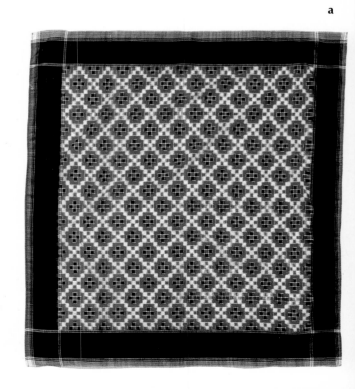

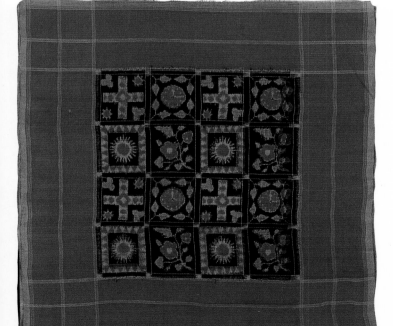

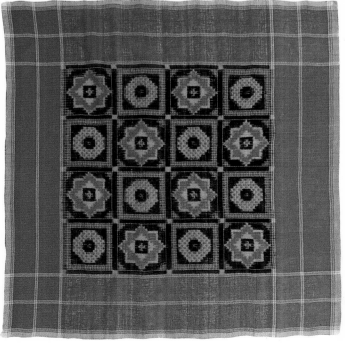

b

c

Quilted and embroidered 'rumal' (cover) with cowrie shells, of the Banjara tribe, Madhya Pradesh

(Opposite) Banjara tribe embroidered cover, from Maharashtra or Madhya Pradesh, made of cotton and silk embroidery on a cotton ground

Rumal of the Banjara tribe, embroidered in silk and cotton on a cotton ground, edged with cowrie shells and cotton-and-cowrie-shell tassels, from Maharashtra or Madhya Pradesh

Half section of 'pallav' of a Toda tribe 'putkulli' shawl, from the Nilgiri Hills, Tamil Nadu

(Opposite) Silk double-ikat sari in the patola style, from Pochampalli, Andhra Pradesh

Warping yarn on a board, in Barpali, Orissa

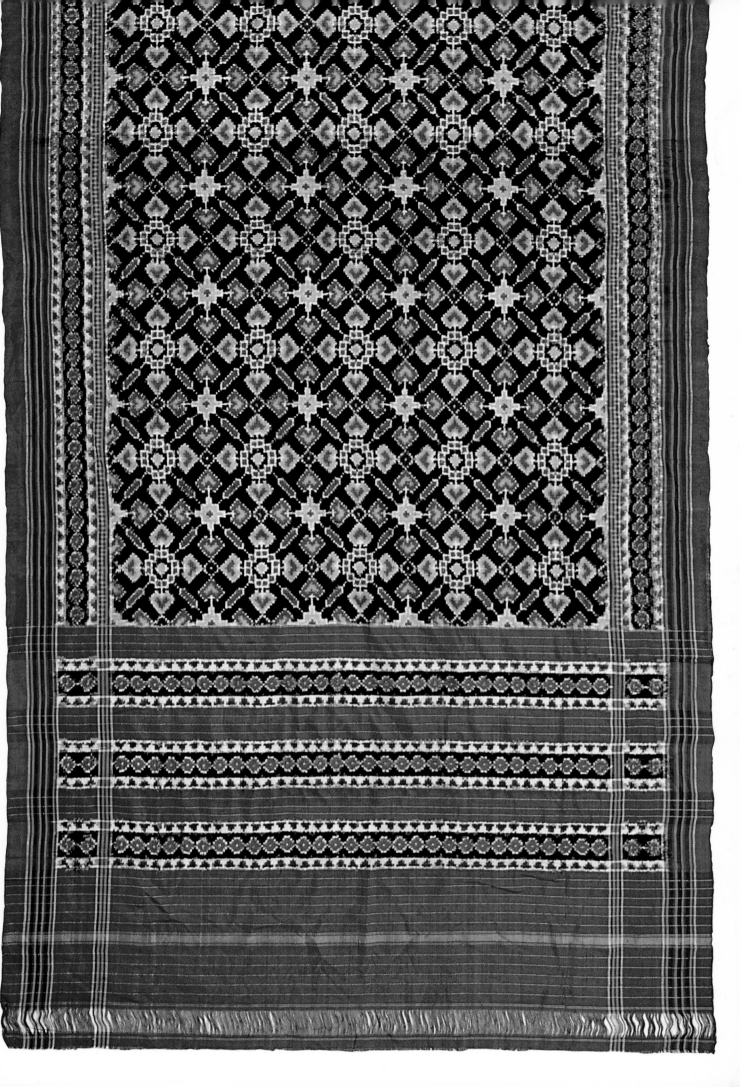

A blanket termed 'tsung kotepsu', by the Naga of Nagaland. Woven wool with a central cotton band painted with figures of 'mithun' bulls, cockerels, lions, tigers, elephants, spears and trophy heads, worn by a prestigious male Naga who has performed the animal sacrifice in keeping with his status

Overleaf: Kantha work on cotton coverlet from Faridpur, Bangladesh

Kantha work 'sujni' (quilt) from Bengal

Silk sari with brocade 'pallav', from Kanchipuram, Tamil Nadu

Guide to Further Information

Bibliography

Barnard, Nicholas, *Living with Decorative Textiles*, 1989
Benn, Elizabeth, 'Bandhani Tie-Dye', in *Embroidery* magazine, vol. 38, no. 4, 1987
Bhattacharyya, A.K., 'Chamba Rumals in the National Museum, New Delhi' in *Bulletin de Liaison du CIETA*, vol. 15, pp. 32–36, 1962
—— *Chamba Rumal*, 1968
—— 'Chamba Rumal – A Pictorial Handicraft of Himachal Pradesh', in Vishwa Chander Ohri (ed.), *Arts of Himachal*, 1975
Broadbent, Moira, *Animal Regalia*, 1985
Buhler, Alfred, Eberhard Fischer and Marie-Louise Nabholz-Kartaschoff, *Indian Tie-Dyed Fabrics*, 1980
Bunting, Ethel-Jane W., *Sindhi Tombs and Textiles: The Persistence of Pattern*, 1980
Butler, Anne, *Embroidery Stitches*, 1979

Cassidy, Rosemary, 'Kashmiri Embroidery', in *Embroidery* magazine, vol. 37, no. 3, 1986
Census of India, 1961, *Kalamkari Temple Cloth Painting of Kalahasti*, II, VII-A, 1, 1961
—— *Kalamkari Cloth Printing of Masulipatnam*, II, VII-A, 1, 1961
—— *Mashru weaving of Patan*, V, VII-A, 11, 1961
—— *Block Engraving at Pethapur*, V, VII-A, 19, 1961
—— *Bandhani or Tie and Dye Sari of Jamnagar*, V, VII-A, 21
—— *Himroo Weaving of Aurangabad*, X, VII-A, 1, 1961
Collingwood, Peter, *Textile and Weaving Structures*, 1987

Desai, Chelna, *Ikat Textiles of India*, 1988
Dhamija, Jasleen, 'The Survey of Embroidery Traditions', *Marg*, XVII, 2, pp. 11–68, 1964
Dhamija, Jasleen (ed.), *Crafts of Gujarat*, 1985
Dhamija, Jasleen, and Mrinalini Sarabhai, *Patolas and Resist Dyed Fabrics of India*, 1988
Durrans, Brian, and Robert Knox, *India, Past into Present*, 1982

Elson, Vickie, *Dowries from Kutch. A Women's Folk Art Tradition in India*, 1979
Elwin, Verrier, *The Art of the North-East Frontier of India*, 1959
Embroiderers Guild, *Indian Textiles*, 1986
Emery, Irene, *The Primary Structure of Fabrics*, 1966
Erikson, Joan, *Mata ni Pachedi*, 1968
Ewles, Rosemary, 'The Ari – A Chain Stitch Tool From Gujarat', in *Embroidery* Magazine, vol. 34, no. 2

Geijer, Agnes, *A History of Textile Art*, 1979
Gill, Harjeet Singh, *A Phulkari from Bhatinda*, 1977
Gittinger, Mattiebelle, *Master Dyers to the World*, 1982

Hacker, K.F., and K.J. Turnbull, *Courtyard, Bazaar and Temple: Traditions of Textile Expression in India*, 1982
Hitkari, S.S., *Phulkari. The Folk Art of Punjab*, 1980
—— *Ganesha-Sthapana. The Folk Art of Gujarat*, 1981

Irwin, John, *The Kashmir Shawl*, 1973
Irwin, John, and Katherine B. Brett, *Origins of Chintz*, 1970
Irwin, John, and Margaret Hall, *Indian Painted and Printed Fabrics*, Historic Textiles of India at the Calico Museum, I, 1971
—— *Indian Embroideries*, Historic Textiles of India at the Calico Museum, II, 1973

Jain, Jyotindra, *Folk Art and Culture of Gujarat*, 1980
Jayakur, Pupul, 'Weaving', *Craft Horizons*, XIX, 4, pp. 24–29, 1959
—— 'Cotton *Jamdanis* of Tanda and Banaras', *Lalit Kala*, 6, pp. 37–44, 1959
—— 'Traditional Textiles of India', *Marg*, XV, 4, pp. 6–36, 1962
—— 'Naksha Bandhas of Banaras', *Journal of Indian Textile History*, VII, pp. 21–44, 1967
—— 'Gaiety in Colour and Form: Painted and Printed Cloths', *Marg*, XXXI, 4, pp. 23–34

Kramrisch, Stella, 'Kantha', *Journal of the Indian Society of Oriental Art*, VII, 1939
Krishna, Rai Anand and Vijay Krishna, *Banaras Brocades*, 1966

Larsen, Jack Lenor, with A. Bühler, and B. and G. Solyom, *The Dyer's Art: Ikat, batik, plangi*, 1976

Marg XV, 4, 1962, *Handlooms*
—— XVII, 2, 1964, *Embroidery*
—— XXXI, 4, 1978, *Homage to Kalamkari*
Mohanty, Bijoy Chandra, *Appliqué Craft of Orissa*, 1980
—— and J.P. Mohanty, *Block Printing and Dyeing of Bagru, Rajasthan*, 1983

—— and Kalyan Krishna, *Ikat Fabrics of Orissa and Andhra Pradesh*, 1974

Nabholz-Kartaschoff, Marie-Louise, *Golden Sprays and Scarlet Flowers: Traditional Indian Textiles*, 1986
Nanavati, J.M., *The Embroidery and Bead Work of Kutch and Saurashtra*, 1966
Nath, A., and F. Wacziarg, *Arts and Crafts of Rajasthan*, 1987
Newark Museum, *The Museum*, vol. 17, nos. 3 and 4, 1965
Nicholson, Julia, *Traditional Indian Arts of Gujarat*, 1988

Paine, Sheila, *Chikan Embroidery, The Floral Whitework of India*, 1989
—— *Embroidered Textiles*, 1990
Peebles, Merrily, *Court and Village. India's Textile Traditions*, 1981

Quick, Betsy, and Judith Stein, *Ply-Split Camel Girths of West India*, 1982

Saraf, D.N., *Arts and Crafts of Jammu and Kashmir*, 1987
Saraf, D.N., *Indian Crafts*, 1982
Sethna, Nelly, H., *Kalamkari*, 1985
Smith, John D., 'Where the Plot Thickens: Epic Moments in Pabuji', *South Asian Studies*, 1986
Spear, Percival, *A History of India Volume 2*, 1966
Stack, Lotus, *Patterned Threads: Ikat Traditions and Inspirations*, 1987
Sutton, A., P. Collingwood and G. St Aubyn Hubbard, *The Craft of the Weaver*, 1982

Talwar, Kay, and Kalyan Krishna, *Indian Pigment Paintings on Cloth*, 1979
Thapar, Romila, *A History of India Volume 1*, 1966

Varadarajan, Lotika, *South Indian Traditions of Kalamkari*, 1982
—— *Traditions of Textile Printing in Kutch, Ajrakh and Related Techniques*, 1983

Welch, Stuart Cary, *India: Art and Culture, 1300–1900*, 1988
Whitechapel Art Gallery, *Woven Air: The Muslin and Kantha Tradition of Bangladesh*, 1988

Yacopino, Feliccia, *Threadlines Pakistan*, 1987

Museums and Galleries with Collections of Indian Textiles

The museums and galleries listed below have interesting collections of Indian textiles, either on display or in store; however, it is advisable to contact museums in advance to determine what textiles are on display. Most textile curators will grant access to their stored collections if an appointment is made.

BANGLADESH
Dacca National Museum, Junction of New Elephant Road and Mymensingh Road, Dacca

BELGIUM
Brussels Musées Royaux d'Art et d'Histoire, 10 Parc du Cinquantenaire, 1040 Brussels

CANADA
Montreal Museum of Fine Arts, 1379 Sherbrooke St West, Montreal; **Toronto** Royal Ontario Museum, 100 Queens Park, Toronto, Ontario M5S 2C6

CZECHOSLOVAKIA
Prague Naprstek Museum, Betlémské Námèsti 1, Stare Mèsto 11000, Prague 1

FRANCE
Lyons Musée Historique des Tissus, 34 rue de Charité, 69001 Lyon **Mulhouse** Musée de l'Impression sur Etoffes, 3 rue des Bonnes-Gens, 68100 Mulhouse **Paris** Musée des Arts Décoratifs, Pavillon de Marsan, 107–109 rue de Rivoli, 75001 Paris; Musée Guimet, 6 Place d'Iéna, 75116 Paris; Musée de l'Homme, Palais de Chaillot, 75116 Paris

EAST GERMANY
Berlin Pergamon Museum für Volkerkunde, Bode Strasse 1–3, 102 Berlin

WEST GERMANY
Hamburg Museum für Volkerkunde, Binderstrasse 14, 2000 Hamburg 13; **Heidelberg** Museum für Volkerkunde, Portheim Stiftung, Heidelberg; **Stuttgart** Linden Museum, Hegel Platz 1, 7000 Stuttgart, Baden Wurtemberg; **West Berlin** Museum für Indische Kunst, Takustrasse 40, 1000 Berlin

INDIA
Ahmedabad Calico Museum of Textiles, Retreat, Shahi Bagh, Ahmedabad, Gujarat; Shreyas Folk Museum of Gujarat, Shreyas Hill, Ahmedabad 380015; **Bhavnagar** Arts and Crafts Museum, Gandhi Smriti, Bhavnagar, Gujarat; **Bhopal** Madhya Pradesh Tribal Research and Development Institute Museum, 35 Shimla Hills, Bhopal; **Bhubaneswar** Orissa State Museum, Bhubaneswar 750014; **Bhuj** The Kutch Museum, by Mahadev Gate, Bhuj, Kutch, Gujarat; Madansinghji Museum, The Palace, Bhuj; **Bombay** Prince of Wales Museum, M.G. Road, Fort Bombay, Maharashtra; **Calcutta** Indian Museum, 27 Jawaharlal Nehru Road, Calcutta 13, West Bengal; **Chamba** Buri Singh Museum, Chamba 176310, Himachal Pradesh; **Gauhati** Assam State Museum, Gauhati 781001; **Hyderabad** Jagdish and Kamla Mittal Museum 1-2-214 Gagan Mahal Road, Hyderabad, Andhra Pradesh; Salarjung Museum, Divan Devdu Palace, Hyderabad 500002; **Imphal** Manipur State Museum, Polo Ground, Imphal; **Jaipur** Maharajah Sawai Man Singh II Museum, City Palace, Jaipur Rajasthan; **Jammu** Dogra Art Gallery, Jammu 180001; **Lucknow** Crafts Museum, Central Design Centre, 8 Cantonment Road, Lucknow, Uttar Pradesh; State Museum, Banarasibagh, Lucknow; **Kohima** State Museum, Directorate of Art and Culture, Kohima, Nagaland; **New Delhi** Crafts Museum, Bhairon Marg, Pragati Maidan, New Delhi 110001; Tribal Museum, Thakkar Bapa Smarak Sadan, Dr Ambedkar Road, New Delhi 110055; **Panaji** Museum of Goa Daman and Diu, Directorate of Archives and Archaeology, Arshivad Buildings, St Inez, Panaji, Goa; **Pune** Raja Dinkar Kelkar Museum, 1378 Shukrawar Peth Natu Bag, Pune 41002, Maharashtra; **Rajkot** Watson Museum, Jubilee Bagh, Rajkot, Gujarat; **Ranchi** Department of Anthropology Museum, University of Ranchi, 8344001, Bihar; **Shillong** Central Museum, Lachumeria, Shillong 793001, Meghalaya; **Simla** Himachal State Museum, near Chaura Maidan, Simla; **Srinagar** Sri Pratap Sing Museum, Laimundi, Srinagar; **Surat** Sardar Vallabhai Patel Museum, Sonifalia, Surat 395003, Gujarat; **Varanasi** Bharat Kala Bhawan, Benares Hindu University, Varanasi, Uttar Pradesh; **Vadodara** Museum and Picture Gallery, Sayaji Park, Vadodara 390002, Gujarat

JAPAN
Osaka National Museum of Ethnology (Kokuritsu Minzokugaku Hakubutsukan) 23–17 Yamadaogawa, Suita-Shi, Osaka, Kanebo Museum of Textiles, 5–102 Tomobuchi-Cho, 1-Chome, Miyakojima-Ku, Osaka

NETHERLANDS
Amsterdam Museum of the Royal Tropical Institute, Linnaeusstraat 2, 1092AD Amsterdam; **Leiden** National Museum of Ethnography, Steenstraat 1, 2300 A.E. Leiden

PAKISTAN
Karachi National Museum of Pakistan, Burns Garden, Karachi; **Lahore** Lahore Museum, Sharah-e-Quaid-e-Azam, Lahore; Museum of Folk Arts of Punjab, Lahore

POLAND
Warsaw Asia and Pacific Museum (Muzeum Asji I Pacyfiku), Galeria Nusantary ul.Nowogrodska 18a, Warsaw

PORTUGAL
Lisbon Museum of Overseas Ethnography, Lisboa, Rua das Portas de Santo Antao, Lisbon

SWITZERLAND
Basle Museum für Volkerkunde, Augustinergasse 2, 4001 Basle; **St Gallen** Volkerkundliche Sammlung, Museumstrasse 50, 9000 St Gallen; **Zurich** Volkerkunde Museum der Universität, Pelikanstrasse 40, 8001 Zurich

UNITED KINGDOM
Bradford Cartwright Hall, Lister Park, Manningham, Bradford; **Bristol** Bristol City Museum, Queen's Road, Bristol BS8 1RL; **Cambridge** University Museum of Archaeology and Ethnology, Downing St, Cambridge; **Durham** Gulbenkian Museum of Oriental Art, University of Durham, Elvet Hill, Durham DH1 3TH; **Edinburgh** Royal Scottish Museum, Chambers Street, Edinburgh EH1 1JF; **Halifax** Bankfield Museum, Akroyd Park, Halifax HX3 6H6; **Leicester** Leicestershire Museum and Art Gallery, New Walk, Leicester; **London** British Museum, Department of Oriental Antiquities, Great Russell Street,

London WC1B 3DG; Embroiderers' Guild, Apartment 41a, Hampton Court Palace, East Molesey, Surrey; Horniman Museum, Forest Hill, London SE23 8PQ; Museum of Mankind, 6 Burlington Gardens, London W1X 2EX; Victoria and Albert Museum, Cromwell Road, South Kensington, London SW7 2RL; **Manchester** The Whitworth Art Gallery, University of Manchester, Manchester M15 6ER; **Nottingham** Museum of Costume and Textiles, 51 Castle Gate, Nottingham NG1 6AT; **Oxford** Ashmolean Museum, Beaumont Street, Oxford OX1 2PH; Pitt-Rivers Museum, South Parks Road, Oxford OX1 3PP

UNITED STATES

Berkeley Lowie Museum of Anthropology, Kroebber Hall, Bancroft Way, University of California, Berkeley, CA; **Boston** Museum of Fine Arts, 465 Huntington Ave, Boston, MA; S.P.N.E.A., Harrison Gray Otis House, 141 Cambridge St, Boston, MA; **Cambridge** Peabody Museum of Archeology and Ethnology, Harvard University, 11 Divinity Ave, Cambridge, MA; **Chicago** Art Institute of Chicago, Michigan Ave at Adams St., Chicago, IL; Field Museum of Natural History, Roosevelt Rd at Lakeshore Drive, Chicago, IL; **Cincinnati** Cincinnati Museum of Fine Art, Eden Park, Cincinnati, OH; **Cleveland** Cleveland Museum of Art, 11150 East Boulevard, Cleveland, OH; **Denver** Denver Art Museum, 100 West 14th Ave, Parkway, Denver, CO; **Detroit** Detroit Institute of Arts, 5200 Woodward Ave, Detroit, MI; **Indianapolis** The Indianapolis Museum of Art, 1200 West 38 St, Indianapolis, IN; **Los Angeles** Los Angeles County Museum of Art, 5905 Wilshire Boulevard, Los Angeles, CA; Mingei International Museum of Folk Art, 4405 La Jolla, Village Drive, La Jolla, CA; Museum of Cultural History, University of California, 405 Hilgard Ave, Los Angeles, CA; **Newark** Newark Museum, 43–49 Washington Street, Newark, NJ; **New York City** American Museum of Natural History, 79th Street & Central Park West, New York City, NY; Brooklyn Museum, 188 Eastern Parkway, Brooklyn, New York City, NY; Cooper Hewitt Museum of Design, Smithsonian Institution, 5th Ave at 91st St., New York City, N.Y.; Metropolitan Museum of Art, 5th Ave at 82nd St, New York City, N.Y.; **Philadelphia** Philadelphia Museum of Art, Parkway at 26th St, Philadelphia, PA; **Salem** Peabody Museum of Salem, East India Square, Salem, MS; **San Francisco** M.H. de Young Memorial Museum, Golden Gate Park, San Francisco, CA; **Seattle** Historic Costume and Textile Collections, University of Washington, Seattle, WA; National Museum of Natural History, Seattle Art Museum, Volunteer Park, Seattle, WA; **Washington** National Museum of Natural History, Smithsonian Institution, Washington, DC; Textile Museum, 2320 S Street NW, Washington, DC.

U.S.S.R.

Leningrad Peter the Great Museum of Anthropology & Ethnography, 3 Universitetshaya Naberezhnaya, Leningrad

Glossary

ABA Tunic-shaped dress worn by Muslim women over trousers.

ABLA Mirrored glass.

ABOCCHNAI A wedding shawl, embroidered in silk or cotton with motifs of flowering bushes on a red, white or brown cotton ground by the Dars and Pali landowning and the Lohana and Memon merchant castes in Thar Parkar, Sind. Examples of these shawls can also be found in Banni Kutch.

ABOTI A caste of Brahmin farmers of Saurashtra.

ADAI A Jacquard-like device used in Kanchipuram.

AHIR A caste of Hindu pastoralists and farmers. Ahir women of Kutch and Saurashtra are prolific embroiderers.

AJARAKH Cloth, of predominantly indigo colouring, block-printed (usually on both sides) with geometric patterning in Sind, western Rajasthan and Kutch. Worn by Muslim men in these districts as turbans and/or lungis.

ALPONA Ritual floor pattern, drawn at festival times in Bengal.

AMBADEVI Mother goddess worshipped in Gujarat.

ARI A small awl with a notch near the point, used (in the manner of the European tambour hook) to embroider in chain stitch.

BAGH (lit. 'garden') A Punjabi woman's shawl worn at weddings and some other ceremonies. Embroidered in 'heer' (floss) silk so that the background 'khaddar' (handwoven) cloth is almost completely covered.

BALUCHAR A type of silk brocade sari produced in the Murshidabad district of West Bengal in the 18th and 19th centuries, with supplementary weft motifs of diagonal rows of small flowers worked on the central field and in the same technique vivid depictions of warriors, aristocrats, ships, carriages and cannon on the 'pallav' endpieces. True Baluchar saris have not been made since about 1900, but copies made in the traditional manner have been produced at Varanasi since the mid-1950s.

BANDHANI (also bandhej) The Gujarati word for the resist technique of tie-and-dye.

BANIA Common term for a Hindu shopkeeper, merchant or money-lender.

BANJARA A tribe of north Indian origin who are reputed to have moved south to the Deccan plateau when transporting the baggage train of Aurangzeb's invading army. Their traditional caste occupation was carting. Now they are classed as gypsies and sometimes as farmers. Banjara women produce some of the most intricately stitched folk embroidery in all India.

BARI A 'toran' (embroidered doorway hanging) in the shape of an arch. From Kutch and Saurashtra.

BESAN (also bhitiya) An embroidered, appliquéd or beadwork hanging which is hung right across the walls of Kathi houses in Saurashtra.

BHANSALI A caste of Hindu farmers who are largely settled in Kutch but can also be found in Saurashtra and the rest of Gujarat.

BHARWAD A caste of herders found in Kutch and Saurashtra.

BHATTIA A caste of Hindu traders who are mainly centred on Kutch.

BHITIYA See BESAN.

BHOPA Itinerant performer, sometimes accredited with shamanistic powers.

BISHNUI Hindu herding caste of western India, followers of twenty-nine (bishnui) sacred precepts. Vegetarians, noted for their care of wildlife.

BRAHMIN Members of the highest priestly caste whose men wear the sacred thread.

BUKHANI Scarf or sash, worn by bridegrooms in Kutch and Saurashtra and Thar Parkar, Sind.

BUTTI Flower design in textiles. The 'Paisley' cone design of Kashmir is also termed 'butti'.

CHAKLA A square hanging (embroidered, appliquéd or of beadwork) from Kutch and Saurashtra.

CHANDARVO A large, usually square, embroidered, appliquéd or block-printed cloth used as a canopy at marriages and other ceremonies in Gujarat and western Rajasthan.

CHARAN A pastoral caste of western India, once bards to the local courts.

CHAUHAN A caste of Muslim carters found in Sind, whose patchwork quilts are noted for their beauty.

CHINAI Silk embroidery on silk produced by Chinese embroiderers in Surat during the 19th and early 20th centuries, depicting Chinese motifs and using Chinese techniques.

CHOPE A 'phulkari' shawl made by the maternal grandmother of a Punjabi girl for presentation at her wedding. The chope is embroidered with a type of double darning stitch so that the design will appear identical on both sides of the shawl.

DARGAH Shrine and tomb of a Muslim saint.

DARS Landowning caste of Sind.

DHARANIYO (also darnia, orchar) Rectangular embroidered or appliquéd cloth used in Kutch and Saurashtra to cover a pile of quilts when they are not in use.

DHARMSALA Rest house for Hindu pilgrims.

DHOTI A rectangular length of cotton cloth (usually approximately four yards long and made of thin muslin) which is tied to form a loose pair of trousers. Worn by Hindu men.

DUPATTA Headscarf for women made up of two breadths of fabric sewn together. Nowadays usually worn draped over the shoulders rather than the head.

ERI A type of wild silk produced mainly in Assam, West Bengal and neighbouring states.

GAGHRA Full skirt worn by women of western India.

GANESH Elephant-headed god. The remover of obstacles, worshipped by Hindus before undertaking any fresh venture.

GANESHTAPAN Pentagonal embroidered hanging with images of Ganesh and his wives Siddi and Buddhi, usually hung on the wall of farming houses in Saurashtra for ceremonial occasions.

GARCHOLA (lit. 'house garment') Red cotton sari with a grid-like pattern of gold and silver brocade-work in which are set tie-and-dye dot motifs of women, elephants, flowers, etc.

GHUGHI A triangular embroidered or appliquéd cover which fits over the ears and neck of a horse.

GOKUL ASHTEME Krishna's birthday.

GOPI Milkmaid.

GUJ Embroidered wedding blouse or coat in Sind and Kutch.

GULBADAN Silk warp-faced cloth in a multicoloured, vertically striped design. Worn as a turban or sash in Sind, west Rajasthan and Banni Kutch.

HAVELI Mansion of a rich merchant or landlord in western India.

HEER Term used for floss silk in western India.

IKAT Woven fabric in which the pattern is tied and dyed before weaving.

JAJAM Floor spread.

JAKH Legendary horsemen, now deified, who liberated Kutch from tyrannical rule in the 10th century.

JALA The thread Jacquard used in brocade weaving.

JALI An openwork pattern in chikan work.

JAMDANI Fabric of fine cotton muslin woven at and near Dacca, eastern Bengal (now the capital of Bangladesh), at Tanda, Uttar Pradesh, and at Varanasi.

JHUL An embroidered or appliquéd cover for a bullock's back.

JOGI A caste of snake charmers or snake catchers found in Sind and Kutch. Jogi women of Badin district, Sind, stitch quilts to a unique design.

JULLAHA Weaver.

KADWA An important branch of the Kanbi farming caste. Found in southern and central Saurashtra.

KALABATTUN Silver gilt thread used for brocading and embroidery.

KALAM Pen-like instrument made of either bamboo or iron with a felt-like reservoir near the tip, used for drawing out the designs or applying the wax resists for the kalamkari cloths of Masulipatnam and Kalahasti in Andhra Pradesh.

KALAMKARI Penwork hand-painted cloths of Masulipatnam and Kalahasti. (NB Much of the Masulipatnam production is in fact block-printed, but the cloths are still known as kalamkaris.)

KAMEEZ Shirt-like tunic of north India and Pakistan. Usually worn over salwar (baggy pantaloons).

KANBI Farming caste of Kutch and Saurashtra. Kanbi women are the most prolific embroiderers in this area.

KANDURI (lit. 'tablecloth') Name of appliquéd shrine cloths offered to the shrine of Salar Masud at Bahraich, Uttar Pradesh.

KANNADA Language of Karnataka State.

KANTHA Cotton cover embroidered by women of Bengal on quilted layers of old discarded dhotis or saris.

KARIGAR (lit. 'artist') A brocade weaver of Varanasi.

KARKHANAH Workshop, particularly of the Mughal period.

KASUTI Embroidery work of north Karnataka and the adjoining Kannada-speaking districts of Maharashtra. Figurative designs are worked in cross stitch and a variety of running stitches.

KATAB Gujarati term for appliqué.

KATHI Landowning caste of Saurashtra.

KATHIPA A style of embroidery in 'heer' (floss) silk, utilizing geometric designs with adjoining areas of the design achieving a variation in texture by working one section in the horizontal direction, the other in the vertical, in the manner of Punjabi bagh embroidery.

KERIYA A tight-fitting, long-sleeved jacket with a skirt-like border flaring out from breastbone level. Worn by young children, adolescent boys and grown men in Gujarat.

KHADDAR (also khadi) Handspun, handwoven cotton cloth.

KHATRI A caste of professional dyers.

KHATWA Appliqué work of Bihar. The design is cut out of a whole piece of cloth which is then stitched to the background cloth. The term also applies to a method of Lucknow chikan work whereby sections of fine fabric are appliquéd underneath semi-transparent fabric.

KINKHAB Heavy silk fabric brocaded with silver and gold and used mainly for furnishings. Varanasi is the traditional production centre for kinkhab cloths.

LAKSHMI Hindu goddess of wealth.

LEHERIA (also laharia; lit. 'waves') A resist-dyeing technique, which results in a multi-striped or chequered, multicoloured patterning.

LOHANA Hindu merchant caste of Sind and Kutch.

LUNGI Man's sarong-like unstitched nether garment.

MAAN Main room of a Kathi house.

MAFFA An appliquéd tent-like cover for an ox cart used at marriages and other celebrations by some farming castes in Kutch and Saurashtra.

MAHAJAN Gujarati merchant or moneylender.

MALDHARI Cattle traders in western India.

MALIR Cotton cloth of Sind and western Rajasthan woven on narrow looms, block-printed in the ajarakh style, but mainly in red rather than indigo blue. Originally printed in the Thar Parkar village of Malir, although now printed in other places in Sind, and in Barmer, Rajasthan.

MANDAP Gujarati wedding pavilion.

MARWARIS (lit. 'inhabitants of Marwar', the old name for Jodhpur state) Members of the Rajasthani trading caste, which is now the dominant force in business and industry throughout India.

MASHRU (lit. 'permitted') A warp-faced textile of mixed fabric, silk (now usually synthetic) warp and cotton weft.

MASNAD Cloth floor covering.

MATH Monastic house in Puri, Orissa.

MEGHWAL (also Meghwar) A caste of leather workers found in Sind, Banni Kutch and western Rajasthan.

MEHR A farming caste settled mainly in western Saurashtra.

MEMON A Muslim merchant caste of Gujarat and Sind.

MISRU (lit. 'mixed') Refers to the fabric more generally known as 'mashru'.

MISTRI Artisan, most generally a carpenter.

MOCHI Male professional embroiderers of Kutch and Saurashtra, famed for their delicate ari-work silk embroidery.

MOLESALAAM A Muslim landowning caste of Saurashtra.

MORDANT A metallic salt which combines chemically with the dyestuff to fix the dye permanently.

MOTI Glass beads, particularly Venetian Murano beads.

MURANO The island in the lagoon of Venice that has been the centre of Venetian glassmaking since 1292.

NAKSHA BANDHA Master craftsmen of Varanasi who tie the naksha or jala for the weaving of 'Benares' brocades. Akin to the western Jacquard, the naksha is an arrangement of threads that, when fixed on to the loom, enables the weaver to lift the required warp threads to produce the desired design on the fabric.

NAKSHI KANTHA A kantha with elaborate pictorial embroidery, rather than a simple stitched non-representational kantha.

NAYAK A caste of bhopas who perform the Pabuji epic in Rajasthan.

ORCHAR *See* DHARANIYO.

OSWAL (BANIA) A caste of Jain merchants.

PACHHITPATI Gujarati embroidered frieze.

PALLAV Decorated endpiece of a sari.

PAT Cloth length in Gujarat. Pat means 'floss silk' in Punjab.

PATOLA Famous double-ikat silk saris now woven only at Patan, Gujarat, but formerly also at Surat and other towns.

PHIREN Woollen smock worn by Kashmiris.

PHULKARI (lit. 'flower work') Shawls of khaddar cloth worked by Punjabi women in cloth silk, leaving much of the background cloth unembroidered.

PUGRI Turban.

PURDAH (lit. 'curtain') The custom of the seclusion of women.

PUTALI Figure of a woman or doll.

RAJPUT Warriors by caste, the former ruling class of west India.

RAVANA Mythical many-headed demon king of Lanka.

RAVANHATTHA Stringed fiddle-like instrument played by a bhopa in Rajasthan whilst narrating the Pabuji epic.

RUDRAKSHA (lit. 'tears of Shiva') Seeds of the Javanese tree *Eleaocarpus ganitrus*, revered and used in India as necklaces and rosaries by Shiavite priests, holy men and devotees.

RUMAL Either a kerchief worn over shoulders or head, or a square cover for gifts or food.

SADLO Gujarati woman's wrap, worn over petticoat and blouse in the manner of a sari.

SAKTAPAR Sari with a chequerboard design in the central field, woven in single and double ikat at Sambalpur, Orissa.

SALAR MASUD A nephew of Mahmud of Ghazni (the first Muslim invader of India, d. 1033/34). A cult developed around his tomb at Bahraich, Uttar Pradesh, with both Muslim and Hindu devotees. This involved the offering of appliquéd cloths known as 'kanduri' as covers for the tomb.

SALWAR Baggy trousers worn in north India and Pakistan.

SEBAK Artisans engaged on a regular basis to supply articles for rites at the Jagannath temple at Puri, Orissa.

SEBAS Rites performed at the Jagannath temple, Puri, Orissa.

SHISHA Mirrored glass used in embroidery work.

SISUM A type of rosewood; *Dalbergia roxburgh*, used in the making of furniture and wooden printing blocks.

SODHI A Rajput clan.

SUJANI The name in north Bihar for kantha-like quilting and stitchery.

SUJNI A quilt in the kantha work of Bengal.

SUTTEE The immolation of a widow (usually a Rajput) on her husband's funeral pyre. This practice has been illegal in India since 1829.

TALUKA District of administration in India.

TANGAIL Town near Dacca, Bangladesh. In India, jamdani saris woven in west Bengal are known by the trade name 'Tangail'.

TANGALIA Woman's woollen loin cloth of the Bharwad caste, Saurashtra.

TELIA RUMAL Square double-ikat headcloth or loin cloth from Andhra Pradesh.

TEPCHI Chikan-work stitch.

TODA Tribe of pastoralists centred around Ootacamund in the Nilgiri hills, Tamil Nadu.

TORAN Gujarati doorway hanging.

ZAMINDAR Landlord.

ZARI Metal thread embroidery.

Sources of Illustrations

Colour Illustrations
All studio photography is by **Sian Davies**, with the exception of the photographs which appear on the following pages: p. 112, reproduced by kind permission of **Sheila Paine**; pp. 22, 23, 53, 54 (odhni), 70 (odhni), 72 (choli), 100 (toran), 101 (sankhtoran), 108 (detail of sleeve), 110, 111, 139, 143 and 146 (pallav), by **Ian Skelton**; and pp. 26–7 (sample cloth), 52–3 (chamba rumal), 103 (double-ikat patola sari) and 137 (mashru yardage), reproduced by courtesy of the Board of Trustees of the **Victoria and Albert Museum**.

Location photography: pp. 54 (preparing the dye bath), 103 (Muslim women) and 108, by

Peter Ackroyd; pp. 43 (Ishwar Singh), 44, 46 (woodblock-carving), 48 (Khatri dyer and cloth), 50 (sari-weaving), 52, 54 (Khatri dyer), 66, 70 (maan), 76, 78 (bridegroom and father), 100 (Ahir doorway), 101 (Ahir interior), 103 (camels), 124 (sheep-washing), 138 (drawing with a kalam), 142 (preparing the yarn, marking out the weft threads, yarn on a dyeing frame), and 146 (yarn-warping), by **Nicholas Barnard**; p. 48 (washing freshly printed textiles), by **Verena Buser-Abt** (courtesy of the Archives of the Museum of Ethnography, Basle); pp. 46 (mural), 81 (Rabari boy), 86 (Rabari father and child), 87, 98 and 104, by **Ilay Cooper**; pp. 46 (woman block-printing), 55 (pachedi painter), 68 (bullocks), 84

(Rabari family) and 106 (Rabari family), by **John Gillow**; p. 41 by **Celia Herrick**; and p. 74 (bhopa) by **John Smith**.

Black-and-white Illustrations
Photographs on pp. 9, 10, 11 and 15 reproduced by kind permission of the Royal Commonwealth Society.
All line drawings by Judy Blake, with the exception of: deer motif, from a Gujarati brocade (p. 1), borders (pp. 14, 36, 57, 113, 129, 132), animal trappings (p. 64), by Bryan Sentance. Botanical drawings (p. 35) reproduced by kind permission of the Royal Botanic Gardens, Kew.

Index

Index